# How to Defend Yourself Against Alien Abduction

An exploration of resistance techniques that can be used to prevent so-called UFO alien abduction, a phenomenon being reported in increasing numbers by credible witnesses throughout the Western world. Usually associated with the UFO phenomenon, research now reveals the abductors might possibly be interdimensional creatures from outside our space-time or "hidden" within our own world—creatures reported in religious writings, legends, and folklore in every world culture down through the millennia, and alive and active today.

# How to Defend Yourself Against Alien Abduction

ANN DRUFFEL

Three Rivers Press
NEW YORK

Published by Three Rivers Press, a division of Crown Publishers, Inc., 201 East 50th Street, New York, New York 10022. Member of the Crown Publishing Group.

Random House, Inc. New York, Toronto, London, Sydney, Auckland
http://www.randomhouse.com/

THREE RIVERS PRESS is a trademark of Crown Publishers, Inc.

Printed in the United States of America

Design by Robert Bull Design.

Library of Congress Cataloging-in-Publication Data
Druffel, Ann, 1926–
How to defend yourself against alien abduction / by Ann Druffel.
       p.     cm.
Includes bibliographical references and index.
1. Alien abduction—Prevention—Case studies.   2. Human-alien encounters—Case studies.   I. Title.
BF2050.D78   1998
001.942—dc21                                        98-6414
                                                        CIP

ISBN 978-0-609-80263-2 (pbk.)


145038997

This book is dedicated to Carolyn Henry Druffel, D.C.,
daughter, healer, wonder.

# CONTENTS

# CONTENTS

# ACKNOWLEDGMENTS

This book addresses an extremely controversial subject, and more people have contributed to the manuscript than they realize. I wish to thank all my colleagues in UFO research who, during the past ten years, have provided input for the vital question: Can human beings resist or fend off unwanted contact from so-called alien abductors?

Without recognizing it, many colleagues in the field have answered the question yes or no through their own writings, research, and comments at conferences and other research gatherings. Many more have provided direct input, pro and con, based on their own research with abductees. To all those who offered encouragement during a ten-year quest, I give special thanks. Their friendship has brought joy to the search. Other colleagues, through their questions, steered the research into areas originally unexplored.

Special thanks are due all those witnesses who discovered resistance techniques on their own, shared their experiences and gave permission to include their accounts in this book, and to those researchers who discovered resistance cases and generously shared them.

The following have helped in many different ways: David A. Gotlib, M.D., Dr. Louise Ludwig, John G. Miller, M.D., Alice Nordstrom, Helevi Nordstrom, Dr. David E. Pritchard, Stephan A. Schwartz, Hayden Schwartz, Berthold E. Schwarz, M.D., Dorothy Shapiro, Donald Worley, the late Richard M. Neal Jr., M.D., and all the other members of the Los Angeles UFO Research Group (LAUFORG). And particular thanks to my editor at Harmony Books, Laura Wood, and my friend and literary agent, John White, for their unfailing help and support.

# PREFACE

Thousands of so-called UFO alien abduction cases have come to the attention of researchers in many countries over the past twenty-five years. The majority of these abductions have been reported by demonstrably rational and honest individuals in every walk of life. They have presented a gigantic controversy and many scientists and other professional researchers are avidly studying them.

I regard the cases discussed herein as true accounts of encounters with unidentified beings who are real, at least on some level of reality. The final two chapters in this book will explore the possible nature and motives of these creatures in depth, while Techniques 1 through 9 present sample abduction cases in which the witnesses successfully employed resistance techniques against them.

Because of the controversy in the field, and the fact that skilled researchers have put forth several conflicting hypotheses to explain the phenomenon, many different terms are found in the UFO literature relating to the nature of the creatures and the experiences of the witnesses. I do not favor one term over another. Therefore, "aliens," "bedroom visitors," "harassing aliens," and "visitations" are used synonymously in this book. Likewise, the terms "experiencer," "abductee," and "witness" are used synonymously to describe the hundreds of credible witnesses whose cases have been studied by competent researchers. The terms "abduction," "encounter," and "abduction scenario" are likewise used more or less interchangeably. I do, however, prefer the term "abduction scenario," since it leaves open the possibility that the events are experienced in some type of altered state that science has been unable, up to now, to identify precisely. The term "abduction scenario" in no way detracts from the reality of the event.

# How
# to Defend
# Yourself
# Against
# Alien
# Abduction

# What
# on
# Earth
# Is
# Going
# On?

THE THEME OF UFO ALIEN ABDUCTION is so prevalent today that numerous television programs, such as *Sightings, Unsolved Mysteries, The Unexplained, Strange Universe,* and others have addressed the subject, as well as fictional series such as *The X-Files.* The segments, both fictional and allegedly nonfictional, contain gory details of what human beings undergo at the hands of so-called extraterrestrial aliens. These aliens are most often described as having small, thin, grayish-white bodies with oversize heads and immense oval-shaped black eyes. In fact, so many abductees currently report this type of abducting alien that these particular visitors are popularly known as "greys."[1] We need not even mention the frequent appearance of "alien abduction reports" in supermarket tabloids. Most of those accounts are as fictional as *The X-Files'* version!

On May 19, 1992, the night the second part of the TV miniseries *Intruders* was aired, Philip J. Klass appeared on the CBS eleven o'clock news immediately after the movie ended. Klass has spent thirty-one years in UFO research and has authored six books on the subject, including *UFO Abductions: A Dangerous Game.*[2] He is considered to be a leading UFO skeptic. That night, however, referring to the subject of alien abduction, he stated, "If this is going on, let's stop it!"

He then went on in another sound-byte to explain that he believed all abduction reports sprang from the psychological needs of the witnesses. Psychological needs *are* involved in some reports, but the majority of witnesses reporting traumatic encounters and abduction are rational and honest and seem to be reporting interaction with an unknown phenomenon. Phil's suggestion was appropriate—a logical response to what most UFO researchers consider a widespread human problem. It's as natural as saying, "Drug traffic flowing over our borders is destroying our youth. Let's stop it!"

The only thing we know for sure about the reality of UFO alien abduction is that hundreds, and perhaps thousands, of people in the

United States, the U.K., and various other European countries are reporting similar experiences. Of these reports, a large number come from demonstrably stable, rational persons who at first hesitate to admit they are having, or have had, experiences until they find a supportive UFO researcher to investigate their claims.

In 1966, only two cases of alien abduction were in the UFO literature. The famous case of Betty and Barney Hill, which occurred in the White Mountains of New Hampshire, inspired a well-researched popular book by renowned journalist John G. Fuller.[3] Some years before, a young farmer in Brazil named Antonio Villa-Boas confided to the esteemed Brazilian researcher Olavo Fontes, M.D., that on the evening of October 15, 1957, he had been abducted by humanoids who emerged from a landed, unidentified craft and pressured him into a sexual encounter with a red-haired female alien. At the time of Villa-Boas's experience, such reports were considered very strange, and his account was secretly passed among the top researchers of the day. It was given consideration only because Dr. Fontes had investigated every possible aspect of the case. It was not until Jim and Coral Lorenzen, codirectors of the respected Aerial Phenomena Research Organization (APRO) wrote their 1967 book, *Flying Saucer Occupants*, that the "AVB Report" was given much publicity.[4]

A third early abduction case never published involved the claims of a Nevada woman. In 1965, she reported to UFO researchers that she had boarded an alien craft several years earlier outside the Las Vegas city limits. After traveling with its occupants over several states, she claimed that she was eventually released after allegedly obtaining specific knowledge about the propulsion system of the craft. The Los Angeles Subcommittee of the National Investigations Committee on Aerial Phenomena (NICAP) investigated this case.

UFO researchers of that era generally had time to thoroughly investigate each report that surfaced, whether it be night lights maneuvering erratically, so-called daytime disks seen at a distance, a UFO landing, or other close encounters. Abductee reports were rare. However, investigation of the 1965 Nevada case revealed nothing that could be used to further the cause of UFO research. The woman's specific claims of UFO-propulsion knowledge were checked out by a team of scientists and engineers employed by a major Southern California aerospace company, but they found no data in her sketches and descriptions that could be technologically replicated. The case was quietly put aside.[5]

Something happened in 1973, however, that knocked the UFO research field on its ear, where it has been residing ever since. A flap of abduction reports began with the famous case of Charles Hickson and Calvin Parker in Pascagoula, Mississippi. The UFO field was confounded as abduction reports recounted by demonstrably honest and reliable persons continued to increase exponentially. By 1981, such reports had taken precedence over mere sightings of craftlike UFOs seen at a distance, and the energies of most researchers became concentrated on abduction cases. Throughout the 1980s, thousands of such reports flooded into UFO research organizations and onto the desks of investigators, who were unable, by that time, to pay adequate attention to all that came to their attention. The flood intensified even more in the 1990s, and it continues.

At first the reports were simple accounts of abductions by alien beings; strange, unexplained physical examinations by the aliens; and sometimes conversations on various subjects between abductors and abductees. In most of these experiences, the witnesses were awakened from sleep by the presence of the alien(s) in their bedroom and transported into a UFO-type environment in a trancelike, paralyzed state. A smaller number of experiences reportedly occurred outdoors, with the abductee witnessing a bright light or craftlike object, but also feeling paralyzed and in a trancelike state.

## HOW TO DEFEND YOURSELF AGAINST ALIEN ABDUCTION

Slowly, conscious-recall interviews began to be augmented by the use of hypnosis regression, by which researchers hoped to retrieve additional details. The full story of the Hills' New Hampshire abduction in 1961 had been recalled a few years later in hypnosis sessions, when they were being treated for traumatic aftereffects by a well-known Boston psychiatrist, Dr. Benjamin Simon. When hypnotists, trained and untrained alike, began to attack the problem of abduction reports, the claims began to snowball into far more complicated accounts. Claims of "alien implants" (presumably for the purpose of tracking the witnesses from afar) began to surface. These were soon joined by claims that aliens had either impregnated female witnesses themselves or had planted alien/human fetuses in the wombs of abductees. As the details of abductions snowballed under hypnotic regression, experiencers reported that they had been pregnant (assumedly impregnated by the aliens), but now their fetuses were missing.

Claims quickly followed that these missing fetuses had been removed by aliens during subsequent abductions and developed into full-term "hybrid babies" on other planets. Following this, witnesses began to make allegations that they were at times taken to bond with their hybrid children for the purpose of teaching the emotionless offspring how to respond emotionally to them. These accounts gradually led to claims by abductees that a hybrid race was being produced to take over the earth, either because our planet was due to suffer a catastrophe in the near future that would wipe out existing human life, or, alternatively, because the aliens were from a dying planet and needed a new home on which to survive. The motives of the abductors remained uncertain; some researchers contended that the aliens were using this method to save the human race from total extinction, while others contended that the aliens didn't give a snap for the human race and were only thinking about saving themselves.

Careful study of books written during the 1980s clearly shows a progression of details lacking in earlier accounts. What they do *not* show is that most UFO researchers who wrote these books had little or no recognition that the hypnosis process often establishes a telepathic link between the hypnotizer and the person who is hypnotized. Many of these researchers act as the hypnotists themselves, or at least closely monitor the hypnosis sessions. Even those researchers who are well-educated and experienced do not seem to recognize the possibility that they might be retrieving information from their witnesses that fits into their *own* theories about the meaning of the UFO abduction phenomenon and the motives of the abductors. Thus, one veteran researcher would retrieve accounts of hybrid babies being produced to take over our earth and another would retrieve accounts that the abductors have the best of motives, as claiming to have been assigned by some vague "higher power" to help the human race evolve into greater spiritual consciousness.

It seems significant that Betty Hill never reported an alien transplant or missing fetus, nor did other early abductees. And many of the earlier abduction cases involved creatures that were totally unlike the currently accepted abductor—the small, skinny, large-eyed grey. In the 1973 Pascagoula case the abductors were described as tall, solidly built robotic types, and the entities who interrupted the Hills' journey home were about five feet tall with strong bodies. Their eyes, though large, appeared as though they were wrapped around the sides of their heads, instead of being huge ovals slanted upward, as in most depictions of greys.

The American media, particularly television, presents greys as the main type of UFO occupant. They are not, of course. Descriptions of entities associated with UFOs vary widely, almost as widely as descriptions of the vehicles themselves, and many reports of occupants in and around landed UFOs have nothing whatsoever to do with abduction scenarios.

## HOW TO DEFEND YOURSELF AGAINST ALIEN ABDUCTION

Before the plethora of abduction reports began to flood in around 1973, most cases of "occupants" associated with UFOs involved outdoor sightings in which a variety of different types of humanoids were reported by rational, honest witnesses. These UFO occupants were invariably described as staying near the UFOs, which had landed in isolated areas. The variety of humanoids ranged from near-human types to robots. Most of these purported UFO entities departed quickly from the scene when detected by witnesses. For example, in a well-documented case in Czluchow, Poland, which was reported in the prestigious British journal *Flying Saucer Review*, two shy humanoids, dressed in spacesuits that presumably protected them from the earth's atmosphere, were seen by reliable witnesses.[6] Another example, closer to home, were the two occupants seen in 1965 by a New Mexico policeman, Lonnie Zamora, near an oval-shaped UFO that landed in an isolated gully. These "little people," as Zamora called them, were dressed in white coveralls. When detected by Zamora, he started to drive toward them on an unpaved road. He heard what sounded like a hatch slamming shut just before the unidentified white craft zoomed off into the sky with a loud roar, trailing a brilliant flame.[7]

The reliable witnesses who report UFO occupants seen outdoors generally do not experience abrupt paralysis or trancelike states during the time they witness the craft and occupants. Many objective UFO researchers deem it logical to hypothesize that these occupants are possibly extraterrestrial and wish to avoid human contact. The question of "crashed saucer" reports, like the situation at Roswell, New Mexico (still a matter of much controversy within the UFO field), and the added problem of alleged entities retrieved from crashes muddy the water considerably, implying as they do extraterrestrial visitations.

As details of abduction cases began to converge into two or more theories by prominent researchers, reports of abductor greys became generally accepted. Recently, two other extraterrestrial races have been reported as performing abductions. Along with the greys, "reptilians" and tall, blond "Nordics" were visiting us from the stars, while other types are knocking at the gates.

When questions are raised as to the validity of these cases, those researchers who make such claims invariably respond that some of the accounts they derive from abductees are *consciously* recalled—that no hypnosis was involved. They refuse to acknowledge that many consciously recalled abduction accounts gathered by other researchers contain no mention whatsoever of missing fetuses, implants, hybridization, or other progressive details. Also, they flatly refuse to concede that the relatively few witnesses who give extensive conscious accounts have been exposed to widespread media reports based on hypnotically regressed witnesses.

By the end of the 1970s, I had actively researched about two hundred abduction reports and in 1980 wrote *The Tujunga Canyon Contacts* with parapsychologist D. Scott Rogo.[8] It was the first book to be published on the subject of two-witness abduction scenarios and contained much data pointing to the possibility that abduction scenarios stem from altered-state experiences. Perhaps even more significant, we found evidence of a possible contagious aspect in abduction scenarios, in that one female witness seemed to be the source of abduction scenarios later recounted by four of her friends. Yet numerous interviews conducted with the five witnesses, including hypnotic regressions by a highly trained physician, held no mention of physical implants, missing fetuses, or hybridization. The data we presented in our book countered many prominent researchers' claims that abducting aliens were physically real and belied the widely accepted notion that abductions were physical events (in the sense that they were occurring within the normally perceived space-time continuum).

By the 1990s, the field of abduction research had become unbelievably complex. Added to the accounts of missing fetuses, alien implants, and hybrid babies were claims that alien races were living in huge underground bases on earth and that members of hybrid races were already living undetected among the human population. There were also a growing number of claims that members of the U.S. military were interacting with aliens in secret underground bases, and that the U.S. government was permitting the entities to abduct a certain number of humans each year for their experiments in return for alien technology.

As abduction stories and books became more and more speculative and sensational, the UFO research field seemed headed toward chaos. A few objective researchers, including Dr. David Pritchard of MIT, Richard M. Neal Jr., M.D., and myself attempted to scientifically validate claims of alien implants and missing fetuses. No solid evidence or verification emerged. Each case that was followed to its logical conclusion was proven to be a perfectly normal event. Alien implants were proven to be benign cysts or other explainable occurrences, and claims of missing fetuses were proved to be false pregnancies or explainable gynecological abnormalities.[9]

Some witnesses who have undergone abduction scenarios consider the abducting creatures to be benevolent in nature. Even though they might experience initial emotional trauma and even revulsion toward the abductors, these witnesses become convinced that the creatures' motives are good and that eventually their actions will benefit the world. Some come to these conclusions on their own, and others accept the working hypotheses or theories that abduction researchers share with them.

By 1987, my database of more than two hundred "experiencers" contained only a few who considered the abducting creatures as benevolent, and these did not seem to need counseling or investigation of their claims. They were certain of what had gone on and were happy about it. But others brought their experiences to me as problems, and I investigated and documented what details I could. As the numbers of traumatized abductees grew, it became apparent that something more had to be done. I came to a logical decision: What was the use of piling up more abduction reports while more and more abductees knocked at the door? I turned one of those unwritten laws around backward and decided, "Something's broke; let's fix it."

In 1988, I wrote an article for a leading UFO research journal on the subject of abductee support groups.[10] By that time, abduction reports were so numerous there were simply not enough qualified investigators to handle the volume of cases on a one-to-one basis. Many of the witnesses were so emotionally damaged by their strange encounters that support groups were being formed to help handle the social and psychological problems they were experiencing. In the journal article I separated the abductee population into six groupings in order to make sense of the enormous volume of abduction reports. I'd personally researched cases in each of the six groupings, but realized that classifying abductees involved difficult choices, since each individual was different. However, certain generalizations could be made.

• *Group One* consists of witnesses who appear rational, honest, and socially productive; psychological testing confirms this. They are generally cooperative and open to investigation, but most of them desire anonymity to protect their privacy. Those who are willing to speak out publicly do so without ulterior motives, such as gaining personal notoriety or financial profit. They benefit from reassurance and support by experienced researchers and, in time, are able to assimilate their abduction experiences into their lives with minimum anxiety.

• *Group Two* individuals also seem to be reporting "real events," but the trauma resulting from their abduction experiences causes them more psychological damage than Group One. They have a tendency to become dependent on supportive techniques, sometimes draining energy and time from investigators. However, they are sufficiently stable to recognize this and make attempts to remedy the situation.

- *Group Three* witnesses appear extremely damaged, both emotionally and mentally; their behavior is consistently neurotic. They drain researchers of time and energy to such an extent that normal support techniques are of minimal value. The content of their abduction reports, however, does not vary significantly from Groups One and Two, and it is entirely possible that their experiences are just as valid.

- *Group Four* seems to be psychotic individuals who probably hallucinate or imagine their abduction experiences. Even though a real experience might lie at the core of their statements, their stories are complex in the extreme and new details constantly emerge. These victims are, in essence, psychic vampires, constantly seeking support, reassurance, compassion, and above all, belief.

- *Group Five* is composed of hoaxers who consciously fabricate their stories; they constitute only a tiny fraction of the abductee population, perhaps 1 or 2 percent. Their reasons for hoaxing range from prank-playing to a pathological need for attention.

- *Group Six* surfaced unexpectedly during my review of the more than two hundred abduction cases I investigated personally between 1965 and 1988 and was discussed in one of two new chapters in the 1989 paperback edition of *Tujunga Canyon Contacts*. In my 1988 journal article I wrote: "This group may be large or small—little is known about it and very little has been published in UFO literature concerning individuals of this type. These are fully rational, truthful, and productive persons." Although they report experiences similar in content to those related by Groups One through Three, they differ dramatically from other abductees in that they report *they have been able to break off* the traumatizing experiences and prevent further contacts with the harassing entities by the use of simple mental and physical techniques.

The discovery of Group Six was a revelation. If some abductees were able to fend off the "entities," perhaps further study of the individuals in this group might yield solid evidence concerning two important aspects of the abduction question. First of all, could the personality traits that enable Group Six individuals to resist intrusive entities be identified? Second, could the techniques they used be taught to others? And—an obvious third aspect to this study—could these reports possibly reveal clues as to the *basic nature* of the intruding entities? In other words, if some human beings could fend off intrusive aliens, this might present evidence that UFO abductors were not technologically superior extraterrestrials, as many UFO researchers theorized. The entities might be something else!

I began a study of Group Six with the intent of compiling a database of similar cases, having been advised by scientists and statisticians that at least 200 resistance cases were necessary to obtain significant results. In order to alert the UFO field that this study was being undertaken, I continued publishing data as it emerged in a series of articles that appeared in major UFO publications in the United States and England.[11]

The response to these articles was twofold: Many objective researchers, such as Berthold E. Schwarz, M.D., the late Richard M. Neal Jr., M.D., John Miller, M.D., and others encouraged the study into this new aspect of UFO abduction, and a couple of colleagues, including veteran UFO investigator Don Worley, generously shared documented cases in which witnesses had apparently been able to defend themselves against harassment. Also, many individuals around the country reported their own successes at fending off typical UFO alien abductors. Within three years, my database climbed from a half-dozen individuals to more than forty, and the defense techniques described—all simple mental and physical processes—increased from three to nine! These responses were what I was hoping for to further develop what I initially called "The Fend-off Study."

## HOW TO DEFEND YOURSELF AGAINST ALIEN ABDUCTION

A different type of response to these introductory articles, how-ever, was unexpected; I quickly learned that the subject of resis-tance against UFO entities was controversial to the extreme. Many colleagues in the field, including high-profile researchers, voiced their opinions that defense against UFO alien abduction was impossible. Period. Some informed me that the aliens had merely permitted the witnesses to *believe* they'd broken contact. Others who favored the hypothesis that UFO entities are helping us evolve objected to my study, contending that witnesses *shouldn't* resist. Others felt that abducting entities are extraterrestrials with superior technology; therefore resisting them couldn't work and the wit-nesses were merely fooling themselves or "making up stories." Another colleague engaged in an extended exchange in the UFO literature, contending that because of my research some abductees might try resistance methods and fail, and that such failure would add to the trauma they were already experiencing. Therefore, this colleague charged, encouraging abductees to try resistance tech-niques could be considered unethical.

These specific charges and objections will be discussed in greater depth in following chapters. In the meantime, I would like to point out that successful resistance, as discussed in this book, applies mainly to reports of the type of bedroom visitors termed "greys." The reports concerning this type of harassing visitor are so prevalent that the image of the spindly, bug-eyed creature has entered into modern culture, appearing in advertisements, car-toons, and other popular forms of the media. In the advertising media they are usually portrayed as benevolent or harmless.

As far as the extraterrestrial hypothesis is concerned, sightings of landed UFOs associated with alien occupants—who seem to avoid interaction with humans—might possibly indicate clandes-tine earth surveillance. In some of these, the craft or occupants interact minimally with the witnesses; for example, blinking lights from the UFO apparently answer light signals directed toward the

UFOs by the witnesses. Or, in other cases, the occupants might look at the witnesses curiously for a moment, or make some obscure hand gesture, or in cases where the witnesses seem to come too near too fast, stop them by paralyzing them briefly, just long enough to make their escape. This type of temporary paralysis is reportedly accomplished with some type of small instrument held in the UFO occupant's hand and differs from the generalized paralysis reported by abductees. At least one scientific researcher has hypothesized that it is microwave-produced, rather than associated with altered states.[12]

Contrasted to these shy UFO occupants, who make it plain that they do not wish extended interaction with witnesses, the greys and other abducting entities appear extremely interested in members of the human race. Their extended interactions are, in the words of witnesses, intrusive, harassing, interfering, and unwelcome. While the majority of outdoor sightings with shy occupants seem to be physical in nature, current hypotheses being developed by several objective researchers suggest that the greys might be interdimensional in nature or, alternatively, that they may normally exist in an invisible portion of our own electromagnetic (EM) spectrum. In other words, they might not originate in our *normally perceived* space-time—that is, those very limited portions of the vast EM spectrum that are detectable by human senses.

Both hypotheses speculate that the so-called greys possibly have the ability to enter into our normally detectable space-time and become *temporarily* physical. Both hypotheses, to me, seem to be logical working assumptions. If the greys are truly interdimensional in nature—that is, coming from a space-time continuum coexisting with but separate from ours—this might explain why intrusive human/visitor interaction most often occurs in some type of altered reality, involving an as-yet-unidentified altered state. The same thing might apply if they are usually invisible to us by reason of their existence in normally undetectable portions of our own EM spectrum.

The evidence to date indicates strongly that many abduction scenarios are "real" at some level of reality, since large numbers of psychologically sound individuals report them. The following chapters detail descriptions of nine resistance techniques that have been described by several dozen rational, honest, and productive human beings, plus a couple of other techniques that are in the stage of being investigated. Each case involving the nine techniques has been carefully researched and documented. Some of these resistance techniques are effective when the initial approach of visitors is sensed but before they are visible to the victim. Others are effective after initial paralysis sets in, before or after the visitors have materialized in visible form. Other abductees have attained success even after the abduction is fully under way. One of the techniques can be used *after* an abduction scenario to help prevent the return of the unwanted intruders. And some of these nine techniques are most effective when used in combination.

The main reason for this book is that thousands of people, mostly in the United States (and increasingly in other countries around the world), are reportedly being caught in terrifying situations involving contact with harassing, unidentifiable creatures. Such human beings need help; this book gives both hope and practical help. It demonstrates how dozens of human beings like themselves have been caught in similar situations but have been able to put an end to them. It is only fair to point out again that other UFO researchers, some of them prominent and respected, disagree with the information presented here. The objections of these colleagues will be presented in later chapters' so that readers can judge for themselves where the truth lies.

Even if all abduction scenarios prove to be some type of psychological aberration, as some skeptics and debunkers conclude, the resistance techniques described can still be effective for Group

One through Three. They would also benefit Group Four, provided these experiencers truly wish to defend themselves against further "visits." Individuals who fall into Group One and Two would benefit most, as they are in full control of their own mental states.

I emphasize again that some readers may feel that the motives of the greys are benevolent, or they may have faith in researchers who contend that the so-called aliens are here to "evolve" us. If these readers do not want to try resistance for any reason, they have a perfect right to refuse. I am not trying to persuade them to act against their wills. This book is also meant for the reading public who are simply curious about the widely reported alien abduction phenomenon. But in particular, it is for those who are seeking help in ending unwelcome interaction with unidentified "visitors."

# Resistance Technique #1

---

# Mental Struggle

# MENTAL STRUGGLE

- Effective against the first stages of abduction, particularly paralysis and a general feeling of terror. A high-pitched, irritating sound is at times involved.

- When used at these initial stages, the second phase of abduction—calmness or compliance with the entities' wishes—is prevented.

- A feeling of confidence on the part of the experiencer that the technique will be effective (either from prior personal experience or assurance from a trusted source) is essential.

- A stouthearted feeling that the "intruders" are violating your inalienable rights must be sustained.

- Maintain patience: This technique requires strong, internal, silent struggle, directed toward moving one small part of body, usually a finger or a toe. When movement occurs, the paralysis usually breaks abruptly and the visitors vanish.

- For a few witnesses, the movement of the body parts must be progressive until the paralysis is broken sufficiently to allow the experiencer to call for help.

**M**OST TECHNIQUES THAT ABDUCTEES and other close-encounter witnesses use to defend themselves against unwelcome bedroom visitors are discovered almost by accident. They come intuitively to mind when the need arises. The first technique discovered during my research is also one of the most commonly reported. Because witnesses describe it in more or less the same terms, we call it "Mental Struggle."

It is termed "mental" because, in the first stages at least, it is done silently, within the mind of the person using it. It is "struggle" because it requires a strong-willed person who is convinced that his or her rights are being assailed by the mere presence of the intruding entity. Persons who wish to try this technique should know that other abductees have used this method against harassing entities and have succeeded in fending them off. In using it for the first time, they can feel confidence that, since the technique has worked for others, it is entirely possible that it will work for them as well. The first success at using mental struggle will amplify the abductee's confidence, and the technique might work faster, should the visitors return to try again.

A crucial point in using Mental Struggle is that numerous persons who use it successfully report back to researchers that the intruding creatures almost invariably react with surprise when human beings show resistance. This fact alone indicates that these harassing creatures, whatever or whoever they might be, seem to feed on fear. If a witness confronts them self-confidently with Mental Struggle (or any of the other defense techniques described in this book) the creatures seem powerless against them.

There are, of course, various stages in the abduction process, which differ somewhat from witness to witness. Some abductees sense the approach of intruding entities before any physiological effects are noted. Usually a general paralysis abruptly sets in, rendering the human being unable to move except for slight head and eye movements. Many experiencers, awakening already paralyzed, sense unseen presences around their beds. Although unseen, the presences cause overwhelming terror. Other experiencers awake already paralyzed and terrified to see the entities materialized, fully or partially.

The next stage is often an unnatural "calmness," which also sets in unexpectedly, apparently by some action of the materialized entities. This seems to be connected with telepathic reassurances from the entities, such as "No need to be afraid," "It will be over soon," or "We'll bring you back." The feeling of calmness is emotionally beneficial to many abductees who do not try to resist. If they have had prior abductions, they realize they *have* been brought back, virtually unharmed. Witnesses who experience the calm are not as likely to resist instinctively as those in whom the calmness has not yet set in.

Therefore, Mental Struggle is an effective technique to use when the witness still feels free to use his or her mind to protest against the invasion, even though the witness feels paralyzed and terrified. To describe it briefly, Mental Struggle involves *sustained willpower* while attempting to move some small part of the body, such as a finger or a toe. When the witness succeeds in making that slight movement, the paralysis generally breaks abruptly, and the entities immediately vanish. There is sometimes a strange sense of a "second awakening," which is totally unlike awakening from sleep. It is more like emerging from an (unidentified) altered state into a fully conscious state.

It is worth saying again: Mental Struggle is so defined because it is accomplished silently and involves great internal effort on the part of the witness. Witnesses who report using this technique successfully are usually relatively fearless and have a strong sense of themselves as Persons with Rights. They feel that human beings have the right to be safe from intruders who are bent on harm. This right is akin to the "inalienable rights" described in the Declaration of Independence, the basis of the American justice system. For the purposes of this book, the right not to be intruded upon applies to otherworldly creatures as well as other human beings.

The Mental Struggle technique works just as well for witnesses whose personalities are less than fearless, as long as they have a strong sense of being a Person with Rights. A third important point is that the person using Mental Struggle must have a general confidence the technique will work. This confidence might be hard to sustain for some persons who are impatient. Sometimes the technique works within one or two minutes of mental struggling. At times it takes a bit longer, but confidence that the technique will work must be maintained no matter how long the struggle continues.

A sense of outrage against the entities' violation of the witnesses' human rights must be maintained as well. In maintaining this sense of outrage, it is helpful to regard the creatures as beings who are not superior, technologically or intellectually. There is considerable evidence that some abducting entities are *posing* as superior. Doubtless many abduction researchers *cause* witnesses to believe that the entities are extraterrestrial and, therefore, technologically superior.

The three main keys in using Mental Struggle successfully are:

1. Conviction that the technique will work.
2. Sense of outrage against invasion of your human rights.
3. Inner assurance that the technique works just as well for terrified witnesses as it does for those more fearless by nature.

The technique of Mental Struggle is often discovered instinctively when it is used the first time by an experiencer, but after the first success it is used deliberately in subsequent encounters. It can also be learned by abductees who are willing to try it. The first description of Mental Struggle I heard came from Emily Cronin, one of the five women whose experiences are described in my book, *The Tujunga Canyon Contacts*. In the spring of 1956, Cronin was traveling by car in a mountainous area with her roommate, Jan Whitley. They had been on vacation and were on their way home, wending their way at night along the mountainous Ridge Route in California, also termed "The Grapevine" because of its many twists and turns.

There was a lot of big-rig traffic on the Ridge Route, as it was part of a major route linking Southern and Northern California. The trucks' bright headlights were disturbing to Jan, who was driving, so the two women pulled off the road. Their intention was to sleep in the car until the truck traffic eased. In the back of the car, sound asleep, was Emily's five-year-old son.

At some point after going to sleep, both women abruptly awakened, unable to move. It was as though they were paralyzed. Jan was sitting behind the wheel, with her head resting on the left front window. Emily was curled up on the passenger side, with her head on the seat. Emily remembers seeing a bright light nearby, which she at first thought was from the headlights of a truck pulling into the turnoff. It was not moving, however, and remained motionless, flooding the car with light. Emily panicked inwardly. Her fear sprang mainly from her unexplained paralyzed state, as well as an irritating, high-pitched sound that accompanied the paralysis. She could not see Jan clearly because of her position, but she realized that her friend was not moving and was either sound asleep or paralyzed like herself.

Emily tried to cry out but couldn't make a sound. She was terrified and, as the unexplained light continued to flood the car, began to fear they would be defenseless if someone in the other (presumed) vehicle might be planning to take advantage of two young women in the middle of the night. Emily had a strong sense of herself as a Person with Rights that were inviolable, and she realized she must fight against the fearsome situation, not only the unexplained paralysis but also the apparent impending danger.

An idea came to her instinctively. She would break the paralysis by concentrating on moving one small part of her body, one finger or one toe. She set to work and was able, after some minutes, to move one finger. Immediately her entire paralysis broke and the high-pitched sound ceased. Jan also stirred at that very moment when Emily's paralysis broke, even before Emily could sit up and alert her friend.

Jan, however, had no need to be alerted. She had been fully aware of what was happening, just as Emily had been but, like Emily, was paralyzed and feeling great fear. Although a person of great strength and conviction, no method of overcoming the danger had occurred to her. Emily's concentrated Mental Struggle technique, therefore, broke the paralysis for *both* women. At the exact time they were able to move, the bright light instantly vanished. Without speaking, Jan immediately started the car, pulled out of the turnoff and sped down the Ridge Route, still terrorized.[1] Emily sat silently beside her. It was not until they reached an all-night restaurant at the foot of the mountain that they stopped. There they exchanged their perceptions of what had happened.

By the time I began to research their case in 1975, they were still puzzled about the inexplicable occurrence, but neither had drawn any conclusions about it. Hypnotic-regression sessions in the mid-1970s, conducted by an experienced hypnotherapist, Bill McCall, M.D., revealed that the bright light had been from a UFO, and that three tall, black-clothed occupants with thin, flat faces had investigated the car. Their motive seemed to be mere curiosity about human beings. No data emerged to indicate that any abduction was involved.

The experience on the Ridge Route in 1956 almost immediately set up Emily and Jan for other strange encounters in the middle of the night. These repeated visitations were by short, thin, translucent creatures who appeared in their bedroom and were seen by both women. Their appearance was entirely different from the taller, thinner, black-garbed entities on the Ridge Route. Both Jan and Emily were paralyzed each time the intrusive bedroom visitors appeared, and this paralysis was invariably accompanied by a shrill, high-pitched sound. The creatures would tell Emily mentally that they wanted her to "go with them," and she would answer mentally, "No, I don't want to go with you!" For Emily's strong sense of her inviolable rights included the right not to be intruded upon without permission by *any* type of being, human or otherwise. Jan also experienced terror during these episodes. She viewed the creatures but heard no communication.

When Emily objected to the entities' intrusions, the high-pitched sound would increase in pitch until it became virtually unbearable. Emily realized the only way she could stop it was by concentrating on moving one finger or one toe, the same Mental Struggle technique she had used on the Ridge Route. When she succeeded in making one slight movement, it invariably broke the episodes for both herself and Jan.

In 1958, the corporation the two friends worked for transferred to Santa Barbara, and they moved to that California city to continue their jobs. When the firm went out of business, Emily and Jan moved to a hilly section of Burbank, a few miles from the Tujunga Canyons in California. While in Santa Barbara and Burbank, they were not disturbed by intruding entities. As soon as they moved back to the Canyons in 1959, however, the annoying visitations resumed. Again, Emily's increasingly effective Mental Struggle technique fended them off each time. Emily had by now become more mature and assertive and would mentally demand that the creatures cease the extremely irritating sound. The episodes would end abruptly, with the paralysis, the high-pitched sound, and the entities all vanishing together. Eventually the visitations ceased.

Melissa MacLeod, another Southern California resident, also used Mental Struggle successfully to ward off paralysis and unwelcome presences. During the 1970s and 1980s she repeatedly experienced terrifying episodes during which invisible forms of considerable weight—estimated at fifty to eighty pounds—would jostle her bed or poke her until she awakened, and she would find herself completely paralyzed. Although she could see no forms or figures, the sense of unwelcome, intrusive presences was overwhelming.

She instinctively used Mental Struggle the first few times this happened and, after two or three minutes, would eventually succeed in moving some small portion of her body, usually a finger or a toe. Each time, the small movement broke the paralysis, and the presences vanished instantly. After several experiences, she realized that she was using the same technique used by Emily Cronin, as described in *The Tujunga Canyon Contacts.* Melissa has no conscious memories or any other indications that she has ever undergone a full-blown abduction. However, she has a prior history of two time lapses—or amnesiac periods—in the 1950s, directly associated with UFO-type phenomena.

Her first such experience occurred in the summer of 1953. She and her husband were living in an apartment in Los Angeles. They were newlyweds, married only a few months. One night Melissa was awakened from sleep by a high-pitched, whirring sound, somewhat similar to an electric generator. It was very loud, and she could not understand how her husband slept through the noise. Melissa looked out her bedroom window. The neighborhood was dark and undisturbed, and she could not determine from which direction the sound was coming. As it continued unabated, she tried to wake her husband, but he did not respond, which was unusual because he was normally a light sleeper.

Melissa remembers standing barefoot, wondering what to do as the inexplicable noise continued. She was terrified and helpless. Her next memory is of waking up the next morning and wondering how she'd gotten back into bed. It was as if the experience in the middle of the night had been cut off abruptly, or else snatched from her mind. She attempted to find out what the noise had been by asking several of her neighbors if they had heard it, but no one else had. There was no large generator in their residential neighborhood, except at an abandoned substation about a block away, but it had been locked up for several years and was out of operation.

Her second time-loss experience occurred in broad daylight a few years later. By that time, the MacLeods had two small children and had moved to a house in a hilly section of the San Gabriel Valley. Melissa and a neighbor were watching their young children in Melissa's yard when an immense, blimp-shaped object passed over her house. Silvery in color, it was headed in an easterly direction and flying so low that the women instinctively ducked and gathered their small children around them, as it seemed as though the craft was about to crash. Melissa did not see any identifying features on the object, such as the word *Goodyear*. She also has no memory of what happened *after* seeing the object. Inexplicably, she does not remember whether or not she and her friend ever discussed the incident afterward.

Twenty years later, Melissa began to experience the paralytic episodes, and she repeatedly fought off the frightening invisible presences, using the Mental Struggle technique. Gradually her terror began to subside as she gained more and more confidence that the technique *did* work. It was a laborious procedure, involving tremendous effort on her part, both in sustained willpower and energy. She directed mental energy toward moving a muscle or muscles, a process she finds difficult to describe. Each time the paralysis finally broke, after what seemed to be one or two minutes of struggle, she felt great relief in mind and body and usually went back to sleep without much trouble.

During one episode in the mid-1980s, however, she awoke early one morning paralyzed and saw a black, hooded figure standing at the side of the bed. She felt sheer terror. She then instinctively used an entirely different technique that worked even better than Mental Struggle—so well, in fact, that she never found it necessary to use the technique of Mental Struggle again. This alternate technique, also used successfully by other former experiencers, is described in the chapter on Technique #8.

Another variation of the Mental Struggle technique was discovered by a high-profile abductee whose experience is related in Budd Hopkins's *Missing Time*.[2] In that book he was given the pseudonym Steve Kilburn. His real name is Michael Bershad.

"This UFO stuff, I always knew it was so encompassing," Bershad explains.[3] "I just knew it would affect everything—the way I thought, even when I was a little kid. It had always been in my consciousness that lots of people had had experience with them." When he first spoke with Hopkins on the subject, Bershad told him of an experience he had when he was nineteen years old. He was visiting his family in Pikesville, Maryland, during college vacation and was driving back to their home late at night, about two or three in the morning, after visiting his girlfriend in Frederick, Maryland. He remembered a sensation afterward, like having a dream, that lights had been following his car. This was not, however, a clear memory.

His next distinct memory was of awakening, fully dressed, on the floor of his room, where he had apparently slept for several hours. Afterward, he always was afraid whenever he had to drive that particular mile and a half stretch of road and would basically "hit the gas" to get through it as fast as possible.

Hopkins and fellow researcher Ted Bloecher, who first brought Bershad to Hopkins's attention, obtained the services of two highly trained and objective psychotherapists who retrieved Bershad's hidden memories of that night in four hypnotic-regression sessions over a period of two and a half years. Neither psychologist had any interest in UFO research and, in fact, were not even aware that a UFO event might be involved with Bershad's blocked memory until the sessions were well under way. The sessions brought out details of a full-blown abduction by a number of small entities.

These creatures were grayish-white, "like putty." A faint "line," about waist level, might have indicated clothing of some sort. The texture of their skin looked something like "the color and texture of an art eraser." These aliens, according to Bershad's retrieved memories, were occupants of a UFO that had been following his car down the highway. Somehow, the UFO caused his car to leave the road abruptly and come to rest on an adjacent grassy area. When forced aboard the UFO by the first group of small aliens, Bershad underwent a fairly typical examination by another "team" of aliens, led by an entity who seemed to be in charge and whom Bershad came to regard as "the doctor."

Everyone in the UFO field, including top researchers, who know Bershad personally are impressed with his integrity and his straightforward accounts. He is a fine example of a rational, productive individual whose honesty cannot be questioned, akin to Emily Cronin and Jan Whitley. There is nothing about him that causes objective researchers to wonder whether or not he is embellishing his experience. Even though he grew up and went to college during the '60s and early '70s, he never experimented with drugs or drank alcohol, and to this day does not even take aspirin.

When certain memories were retrieved during Bershad's first hypnotic regression session, he was elated to have some answers to his puzzling experience and memory loss. However, he was in no hurry to continue with further sessions. After his initial exhilaration, his fear of UFOs returned, so it was a long time before he consented to a second session. After the four sessions of hypnosis, he recovered enough details to satisfy his own curiosity.

Meanwhile, the experiences with the abductors continued, and many of these events Bershad now remembered consciously. He also began to realize that he had been harassed by the beings since he was a young child, even though he had no conscious memories of the scenarios that had taken place before his terrifying experience on that deserted Maryland road. Bershad sometimes retained conscious memories of the entities' visits and abductions during the late 1970s and early 1980s, and sometimes he did not. But there were times when he got up in the morning, and he knew *something* had happened—that the visitors had returned for another go-round. He tried not to let the continuing episodes disturb him too much. "I tried to live a productive life, and there's nothing I could do about it," he states, describing that particular period in his life.

Around this time, he also felt that the entities might sometimes be visiting him in his sleep, but might have discovered a way to do it so that it didn't disturb him. This vague feeling was in addition to the consciously remembered, disturbing episodes and the visitations he did not consciously remember but sensed. He describes one time in particular when he sensed their presence in the room. He was lying on his stomach but was too tired to lift his head to see if they had materialized. "I thought to myself, 'Damn it, there they are,' and I remember saying, 'OK, listen, guys, I got to get to sleep and I gotta get up at eight o'clock in the morning. So do whatever you're going to do, but please don't wake me up! Just let me rest!'"

By the late 1980s, Bershad began to resent the continued interference by the beings. In the opinion of most UFO researchers, including Hopkins, "abducting entities" were a superior type of intelligence, technologically and intellectually advanced from humans. This hypothesis implied that there was no defense against them, and for many years Bershad shared that opinion. Once the creatures had "selected" a victim, it was theorized, there was nothing that the abductee could do.

As he grew into his middle thirties, however, Bershad decided that this was not good enough. He became thoroughly fed up with the visitations and the subsequent harassments. He remembers thinking, "I've got to learn how to take control. I've got to call the shots here." But how could he possibly "call the shots"?

Early on, his hypnotic sessions had given him a valuable clue. When he first retrieved the memory of his car being displaced abruptly off the road and of seeing the first entity, he remembered thinking, "I could crush this little guy's head with my fist!" To Bershad's shaken mind, the entity's head resembled a big ostrich egg. As he had this thought about crushing the entity's head, at exactly that moment he was paralyzed. And with the paralysis came the feeling of utter terror, because Bershad realized the entity knew exactly what he was thinking. The utter abruptness of the paralysis gave him such a feeling of helplessness that he came to an immediate conclusion that there was nothing he could do about it. Nevertheless, the knowledge that the entity might be afraid of him, or in a sense helpless before him in particular circumstances, stayed in the back of his mind.

In subsequent abductions, he slowly began, verbally or telepathically, to hurl objections toward the abductors. Sometimes he would curse at them, and their reactions told him that his actions were, as he states, "a little disruptive." It was not that the creatures reacted emotionally, for he never got a feeling of emotion from them. With picturesque candor, he explains, "I just got the feeling that I would put a crimp in their style."

Bershad had always been athletic and physically active, and was used to training for sports. At one time he was a tennis pro. He is currently an actor and has appeared in various movies and television series, as well as on the stage. The training for acting and sports involved both emotional and physical step-by-step processes. "Those types of training prepared me to take over, finally," Bershad says. "I remember thinking, 'OK. I can't rush this experience. I'm feeling terrified, and what I'm doing by feeling terrified emotionally is, I'm dispersing my energy. I'm giving away my energy. I'm giving away my power.' "

Once Bershad figured out what his fear during abductions was doing to him emotionally and physically, he realized he had to learn *not to give in* to the fear. He had to *acknowledge* he was afraid, but still go ahead and figure out what he could do in spite of it. If he could develop a technique that would permit him to retain his energy and use it against the entities, *he* would be in control, not them. He came to the conclusion that the only thing he could do was to "take it one step at a time." Like many of the resistance techniques described in this book, Bershad's was evolving from his own unique life experiences.

"In mastering tennis, you learn to grip the racket a certain way, you move your arm, you move your feet, you shift your weight," says Bershad, demonstrating his words with actions during an interview for this book. "One, two, three, four . . . It has to be *very specific*. And that's just what I did."

By 1984, when he first used conscious control to fend off the entities, he was living in a Los Angeles apartment that had a large window in the bedroom. Somehow, he knew instinctively that the creatures who came in the middle of the night either entered or left from that window, moving *through* the glass in a paraphysical manner. Bershad had become acquainted with a small number of other abductees whose experiences he thought were genuine. One was a woman we will call "Melanie," with whom Bershad shared his plans to "take control." They decided that the next time either of them were bothered by the creatures, they would somehow get to the phone and call the other, and that the one who was called would stay on the phone as long as was needed. Bershad and Melanie worked out everything about the process in advance, including what verbal reassurances would be needed to help the one being visited to stay in control. Bershad also shared his ideas for breaking the paralysis that invariably set in with the approach of the entities, so the one about to be abducted could get to the phone to call the other.

Bershad reasoned if he could move one finger while paralyzed, he could move his hand, and then his arm, and then his leg, and so forth. Then he could get out of bed and walk to the phone. The same process would apply to Melanie, if she would be the next one visited.

It was not too many weeks later that he awoke in the middle of the night, paralyzed, realizing that something had entered the window. The creatures had not yet materialized, but as he explains, "I *knew*. I saw everything but the outline!" There was absolutely no doubt in his mind. He lay there thinking, "OK, my super-objective here is to jump out of bed and call Melanie, but I can't do that yet. I'm trying, but I can't. I'm too terrified to do that yet. So I'll very slowly move my finger. There's nothing they can do to stop me from moving my finger."

Like Emily Cronin and Melissa MacLeod, he was successful in moving one finger. But the paralysis did not suddenly break, as invariably happened for them. It is entirely possible that it did not break abruptly because Bershad did not *expect* it to. Emily and Melissa had discovered the Mental Struggle technique through sheer accident and instinct. Bershad, on the other hand, expected that a step-by-step process would be needed. After he moved one finger, he was able to move his hand, then his arm.

"That's how I eventually got my leg out from under the cover, got out of bed, and went over and called her," he relates. "And I remember standing there by my telephone, terrified, and she answered. And I just said something like, 'Melanie.' And she said something like, 'Are they there now?' And I said yes."

"I know exactly what's going on," she told him using the reassuring phrases they had agreed on. "As long as you need me to be on the phone, don't worry. I'm not going to hang up. I don't care if you're on the phone for the next five hours, until ten o'clock in the morning, and you don't say a word. I'm not going to hang up until you tell me it's OK to hang up."

"OK," said Bershad, still overcome with terror because of the presences in the room. But he stoutly maintained his confidence that he could remain in control of the situation as long as he did not disperse his energy by losing his focus and letting his terror take control. If this occurred, he would lose his power to control the situation. Melanie then slowly asked him a series of questions, which he answered mostly in monosyllables. Finally, he felt that the unseen presence was getting impatient with him. "It doesn't like this," he told her, "and it can't do anything to me as long as I'm talking to you."

Finally, the presence suddenly departed. "I remember thinking, 'It's gone!' It was like, *whoosh*, the veil was lifted, and then I could talk normally," he relates. "I told her [Melanie], 'You know what? The damn thing is gone. The little cowards—get back here!' You know, that sort of stuff."

Melanie inquired if he was sure everything was OK. He assured her that the presence had gone, and that everything about the room and his own reactions was entirely normal. "Thank you for being there!" he told her.

Bershad used this technique, a variation of Mental Struggle, a couple of times during the next year or two, and from about 1992 does not remember ever having another experience. Today he is free from abductions. Sometimes the idea crosses his mind that the creatures, whatever or whoever they were, might still be visiting him and that he has absolutely no knowledge about it. He feels so free, however, that to his best judgment, his method of taking control was effective, and he is convinced that it did, indeed, stop the visitations entirely.

Emily Cronin and Michael Bershad experienced typical night visitations by small, white-skinned entities. There are differences, however. Emily, to her knowledge, was never taken aboard a craft, such as has been described by hundreds of apparently rational experiencers throughout the world; to the best of her knowledge she was able to fight off all of their requests to "go with them." Michael's entities were also grayish-white, "pasty," and possibly unclothed, as were Emily's, although the spindly-bodied creatures she saw had a "translucent" quality as well.

One common belief in the UFO field, and in those portions of the public interested in the phenomenon, is that all greys look alike. The most common conception resembles the large-headed entity with huge, oval, black eyes seen on the front cover of *Communion*, a book that well-known author Whitley Strieber wrote in 1987.[4] This type was commonly seen in abductees' sketches, which were transferred into the UFO literature. From 1987 on, the concept of "alien visitors" as large-eyed greys became widespread in the public media, particularly on television. At present, it is becoming more and more prevalent, even in advertising, where the so-called grey has come to represent the UFO phenomenon in an offhand way. This commonly accepted model of greys is fallacious, however. We must be careful of stacking all reported visiting aliens in one barrel. Most honest abductees sketch their visitors in a slightly different form.

This was true to a much larger degree in the 1970s, when abduction cases began to increase dramatically in numbers. Emily Cronin's, for example, had normal-size eyes, as did the sketches of many abductees in the 1970s and early 1980s. Michael Bershad's sketches show black eyes, which are not much more elongated than large human eyes. It was not until Strieber's book in 1987 that the huge, oval-shaped black eyes began to appear in a virtual flood in experiencers' sketches. It is entirely possible, and even probable, that abductees whose cases are newly reported and under research have been unconsciously influenced by the image of greys that is so widespread today.

Clothed or not, large oval-eyed or not, the grey as well as other types of harassing bedroom visitors can be fended off by stout-hearted human beings who feel that their God-given rights are being violated by unknown creatures who come in the night. The human mind alone is a powerful instrument, as we have seen in the cases of Emily Cronin and Melissa MacLeod. And the human mind, forcing the human body to telephone for help in spite of creatures who paralyze their human victims, as demonstrated by Michael Bershad, is another tool in defending ourselves against "alien abduction." The next technique to be discussed springs from a more primitive base—Physical Struggle.

# Resistance Technique #2

---

# Physical Struggle

# PHYSICAL STRUGGLE

- This technique is effective against initial stages of abduction, before the onset of paralysis.

- The sense of violation of the witnesses' rights must be uppermost in their minds.

- A feeling of confidence on the part of the experiencer that the technique will be effective is not essential if anger against intrusion is so overwhelming that the urge to "fight" is swift and virtually instinctive.

- More deliberate use of Physical Struggle, such as employing weapons such as sharp objects or firearms, adds to the witness's self-confidence.

- The technique can be instinctively employed when entities are already present or used in a more deliberate manner with weapon backup when the entities are seen approaching outdoors.

- The intent should never be to kill or seriously injure the intruders, but to inform them that their presence is violating the witness's right to privacy.

CAUTION: Firearms are not recommended in urban or suburban areas where small children and/or innocent bystanders may be jeopardized.

I N  T H E  S C I E N T I F I C  C O M M U N I T Y,  S C I E N - tists keep their research findings close to the chest and do not let colleagues know the details until the results are published in a referred journal. Only then are their colleagues free to comment in that journal's "Letters to the Editor" column or start projects of their own to replicate or build upon the original findings. Conversely, some set out to prove that their colleagues' results were flawed. This is the scientific method.

The UFO field has always been a bit different, however, for ufology is not yet an established science. If researchers (ufologists) stumble upon a new aspect of UFO phenomena, it is often bene-ficial for them to reach out to their colleagues to see if any data fit the new hypothesis. When I first began to investigate resistance cases I used this approach.

Although most of the new data I collected was from individ-uals who contacted me directly to share their resistance expe-riences, two or three research colleagues came forward spontaneously to share cases in which experiencers had described methods they had used to rid themselves of unwel-come visitors. One of these generous colleagues was Don Worley, an objective and studious veteran UFO researcher living in Connersville, Indiana. During the past several decades he has investigated UFO phenomena—everything from lights in the sky to daytime disks, close encounters to reported landings. Like many others, he is now chiefly involved in studying the abduction phenomenon.

Reading my initial "fend-off" articles, in various UFO journals, Worley remembered that among his hundreds of documented abduction cases a few witnesses had described being able to get rid of the unwelcome creatures, at least temporarily. He sent me copi-ous documentation on three cases. One of the most beguiling was that of Patsy Wingate, whom Don referred to, for reasons that will become evident, as "Patsy the mountain girl."

## HOW TO DEFEND YOURSELF AGAINST ALIEN ABDUCTION

The masculine equivalent of "mountain girl" is "mountain man," a generic term describing a strong, independent, self-sustaining individual who generally lives a more or less solitary life in rugged terrain. Mountain men are known for their ability to solve their own problems, to stay alive amid wild beasts and inclement weather, providing their own sustenance. They live more or less harmoniously among creatures native to their isolated habitat. If you transfer all the adjectives pertaining to mountain men to forty-one-year-old Patsy Wingate of Knoxville, Tennessee, you will have a good idea what her personality is like. The only difference is that Patsy does not live alone. She is married, with three children.

Patsy's case is extremely complex, but Don Worley has doggedly attempted to document each and every UFO incident that Patsy's family has experienced. These include, but are not limited to, her numerous abductions by short, spindly-bodied creatures that fit into the general category presently termed "greys," although the creatures she has interacted with do not have the extremely large eyes that many current abductees describe. Patsy fits the model of a productive human being, who reportedly endured repeated visits from the creatures because she felt helpless in the situation. She learned to cope as best she could, prayed a lot, and tried to live a normal life.[1]

Like many other abductees, her problem is generational. Her mother "had things happen," and her maternal grandmother as well. In her immediate family Patsy was not the only one to have experiences with "creatures who came in the night." Her husband also had encounters with unidentified visitors independent of Patsy's own experiences. He developed a fear of sleeping in the back bedroom of their house, but was not inclined to talk freely to Patsy about it. He adopted an attitude that is typical of many men: He closed himself off emotionally to the problem and lived through his occasional experiences as best he could without sharing the details with anyone. Yet he is well educated, a 1968 graduate of Duke University.

The Wingates' son, Patrick, age nineteen at present, began telling his mother about "spiders" who came into his bedroom when he was four. The spiders came out of a UFO on a golden thread and abducted him through the wall into the craft. The boy told his mother that the creatures had large heads and eyes and their legs had an "M" shape. It is possible that the creature(s) might have been some type of mechanism used to transport the boy paraphysically through the wall. Patsy did not share with Patrick the fact that she was having experiences herself with unidentified entities, but she encouraged him to talk about what had happened to him, thereby helping to relieve his anxiety.

The boy's description of the beings aboard the craft fit the type of small whitish entities she'd seen herself. In a way, Patsy might have felt some relief that Patrick's spontaneous statements confirmed the reality of her own encounters. The fact that the creatures were disturbing her child, however, was vastly upsetting to her. It is a well-known fact in the UFO field that the most traumatizing aspect of abduction scenarios is the helpless guilt adult experiencers feel when they are unable to protect their own children from the abductors.

Her daughter, Layla, at age four and a half, reported experiences with what is known in the field as "Men in Black," generically termed MIBs, an aspect of ufology far afield from the satirical 1997 film of the same name. The sheer complexity of this family's UFO experiences runs the gamut of viewing overflights of strange lighted craft to repeated abduction scenarios.

Patsy's case was active in Don Worley's files for fifteen years, and in the early 1990s, with Worley's assistance, Patsy corresponded and talked with me about her experiences. I was particularly interested in a most unusual method she used one night to drive away the entities. It involved a resistance technique that I will call "Physical Struggle." It can take various forms, depending on the person who uses it.

Patsy does not remember the exact date in winter 1985 when this specific event occurred, but the details are still vivid in her mind. Between 1:00 and 3:00 A.M., Patsy was in bed with her husband. They had moved from the back bedroom and were occupying a bedroom in the front of the house, where her husband apparently felt free from night visitors. However, Patsy did not. She never slept in the dark and had developed a habit of leaving the light on in the living room so that it streamed into the bedroom. Her husband often complained about the light, but it seemed to make Patsy feel more comfortable, and perhaps safer.

Patsy was pregnant at the time and had retired late, after a difficult day. She had not been in bed long when she noticed a second beam of light flooding the bedroom. It came through the adjacent bathroom window, which had been left open. She heard a low, humming noise, which in her previous experiences signified the approach of entities. As she stared, three of the creatures walked out of the beam of light, which was a soft green color on the right side of the beam. The entities' gait struck Patsy as bizarre. As she describes it, "it was as though they were marching in perfect unison." This type of "lock-step" motion has been recounted by other witnesses, such as the description by Betty Andreasson in Raymond Fowler's *The Andreasson Affair.*[2]

The entities who appeared in the beam were the size of kindergarten children, but they had oversize heads. Upon seeing them, Patsy felt great anger at the intrusion. She had not been getting much rest during that particular period of her life and was outraged that she wasn't going to be allowed to sleep in peace. She screamed mentally at the entities, "Leave me alone!" They continued to advance toward her, their legs bending slightly with each pace forward. Patsy's anger increased beyond tolerance. She jumped out of bed and ran toward them, attacking the one in the center, who was slightly taller than the other two. Without thinking, she seized its neck and squeezed firmly. She did not have any intention of hurting or killing it but only wanted to get the idea across to the creatures that she was fed up with their repeated harassments. The entity's neck felt somewhat warmer than human skin. To her astonishment, the thin neck snapped and the entity's oversize head fell onto its back. She heard the sound of its neck breaking.

No one can describe better than Patsy what happened after this astounding development, this unprecedented incident of a human apparently killing a UFO entity, because such entities are widely regarded in the field as technologically and intellectually superior to humans. Here are her own words:

> His neck just broke like a twig. Just—*psst*—like that. And its head fell straight backward. Now the other two got this look on their faces like, "Huh!" What they did was you could see their eyes lift slightly in surprise and their faces had a funny kind of droop look. It was like, "How did she do that?" Like, "How come we couldn't stop her?"[3]

The end of the incident was equally surprising. The entities made no attempt to retaliate for causing their companion's injury or, possibly, death. Patsy herself was convinced she had killed it, for it now seemed unable to move. Synchronous with their subdued expression of surprise, the other two entities immediately held up the one Patsy had attacked. They cupped their hands under its shoulders and backed up, still in unison. They moved into the beam of light, dematerializing as they were enveloped in its glow. The beam then disappeared. Although the source of this beam of light was never visible to Patsy during this incident, she surmised that it emanated from a UFO that was hovering over her house. The low humming noise that preceded the appearance of the light and entities gives credence to her hypothesis.

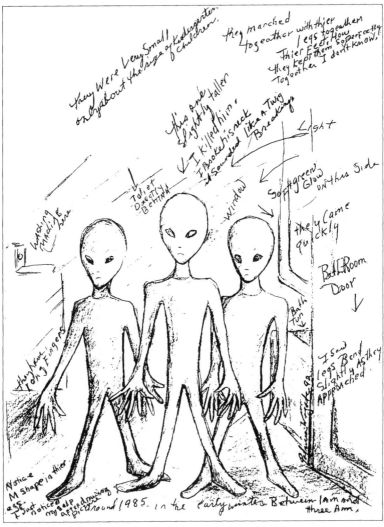

Patsy Wingate's sketch of three entities who entered her bedroom on a beam of light. Angered, the witness jumped up and clutched the head of the middle entity, snapping it "like a twig."

It is apparent that Patsy, at this point, was not feeling paralyzed. It is probable that her anger at the unwelcome visitation was so overwhelming that she felt nothing else. What is all important here is the ability of an ordinary-size human to attack and disable a UFO entity. It shows that Physical Struggle is sometimes possible even in the worst of abduction scenarios, and indicates that the so-called greys are *not* physically superior to humans. We might speculate on two possibilities why that is so: (1) either their own physical makeup is inferior to an average-size human; or (2) their entrance into our ordinary space-time makes them vulnerable in some way, so that human strength, if properly focused, can overcome them. Patsy theorizes that they "travel on light, in contrast to God's angels who *are a part* of the Light," and confirms that, in her experience, their bodies are very fragile.

Patsy points out that she has always had unusual strength in her hands. Her mother used to tell the story that when she was born, the doctor took hold of the newborn's hand to test its grip. "The doctor took hold of my hands with his fingers and I pulled myself up all the way," Patsy states. Increased adrenaline, surging through the human body in response to powerful emotions and causing unusual strength, may also have been a factor here. But Patsy also states that the creatures were fragile compared with humans' physical makeup.

The incident did not cause any vivid emotion in the entities involved—but not so with the human being caught up in the scenario. After the entities disappeared, Patsy went back to bed and lay there for a long time, sleepless, feeling "total remorse" because she was convinced she had killed the creature. Years later, discussing the incident with me, she still expressed remorse. "I never intended to do that," she states. Her compassion and humanity are evident in other incidents she has described to Worley and myself, but in this particular incident she was merely trying to protect herself from uninvited intrusion—a human right to which everyone on earth is entitled.

## HOW TO DEFEND YOURSELF AGAINST ALIEN ABDUCTION

The Physical Struggle that worked so well for Patsy on that momentous night in 1985 is not the only resistance technique she has used against unwelcome night visitors. These will be described in subsequent chapters. The important thing is that Patsy instinctively used a primitive method of self-defense, an ability all humans share.

Physical Struggle is reported more commonly than one might expect. No example I have come across is quite so dramatic as Patsy Wingate's, but any event that involves this particular resistance technique has its own individual drama and importance.

The case of Morgana Van Klausen (pseudonym) is well-known to Southern California UFO researchers; we know her as a hard worker in the UFO field, as well as a particularly objective and rational human being. Morgana is extremely likable, sociable, and talented in many ways. She is an outstanding example of an experiencer who has had several episodes of visitations by unidentified entities and, by employing a *combination* of techniques (some of them used instinctively, others deliberately learned), has kept herself free of unwelcome visitations for the past several years.

Morgana is a talented artist. Her paintings and other artistic works hang in various rooms in her beautiful, spacious home, located in an exclusive section of an upscale city in Southern California. Throughout the 1980s and into the early 1990s, Morgana experienced many various types of UFO phenomena, including silent overflights of huge, triangle-shaped craft with strange lighting, one of which she viewed with her son. She also had several episodes of memory loss as well as conscious memories of UFO-related events.

The type of entity who visited Morgana more than once in her bedroom at night, as her husband slept peacefully by her side, was not the typical large-headed, spindly-bodied grey. Rather, its head was more in proportion to its square-shouldered body. Just below its chin was a red feature that stood out against its black clothing,

*Morgana Van Klausen's painting depicting an entity who paraphysically appeared in her bedroom. (Copyright © Morgana Van Klausen, 1998)*

but strangely Morgana was unable to describe this feature and painted it as only a red mass. During several years of UFO activity, her entire family became affected. On one occasion her husband woke in the middle of the night and saw unidentified "people" in the bedroom. He felt paralyzed and tried frantically to call out to Morgana, but this time *she* slept peacefully through the event. (Mr. Van Klausen, like Patsy Wingate's husband, is not inclined to discuss the episode with researchers.) Morgana's oldest son, whom we will call Quintan, was visited several times by white figures who came through the walls of his closed closet door or, at times, peeked in at him from outside his bedroom windows. In the beginning he referred to them as "clowns," and afterward as "ghosts."

At first Morgana was agitated and worried by the continuing incidents. Her son is intelligent and honest. Morgana saw no reason to disbelieve his statements about frightening bedroom visitors, because she herself was experiencing unsettling episodes. However, she keenly felt her inability to protect the boy. Her guilt was possibly the main impetus behind her decision to rid herself of the intruders.

At first she did not know what to do about the unwelcome creatures who were repeatedly invading her home. She considered the possibility of hypnotic regression but decided against it. She was aware that hypnosis sessions might bring out valid memories, but she also knew that the hypnotized mind is extremely vulnerable to unconscious embellishment and, subsequently, false memories. She decided to seek out help of another sort. She worked closely with me in UFO-related research activities and, being an open-minded person, she gradually accepted the fact that other people around the country were successfully fending off intrusive night visitors. She decided to try it herself.

One night in the 1980s, she was abruptly awakened from sleep to find an entity standing by her bed. It was a type she had seen before and had even painted in oil paints on paper. By this time, Morgana had increased her own natural self-confidence. Although terrified and unable to move, she physically broke through the paralysis and lunged at the creature. Her thoughts were to push it away. As she tried to do so, it dematerialized. She remembers how strange the texture of the creature felt on her fingertips, describing it later as "soft, almost like satin." Even in the midst of her battle with the unknown, her artist's mind was at work, gathering data. The creature's clothing and physical form underneath did not seem to have the solidity and firmness of a typical physical body. It is from such tiny bits of information, gathered from honest, reliable witnesses like Morgana Van Klausen, that scientists and professional researchers may someday be able to bring together information about the true nature of so-called "UFO entities."

Another example of the technique of Physical Struggle against alien abductors is found in the now-classic case of Travis Walton. This totally reliable and well-known abductee is the subject of at least two books, including his initial account, *The Walton Experience.*[4] One of the earliest abduction cases to be thoroughly researched, occurring on November 5, 1975, it differs from the usual bedroom-visitor case in that the initial encounter with the huge, brightly lit UFO was witnessed by six other persons besides Travis Walton. His subsequent abduction and encounter with spindly-bodied creatures aboard the craft fits the abduction scenarios reported by thousands of other rational witnesses throughout the United States.

Since the case is so well known, for the purpose of this book we will concentrate only on the type of Physical Struggle used by Walton when he found himself aboard the huge UFO, after being knocked unconscious by a beam of light that emanated from the craft, in full view of several of his workmates.

The crew had spent the entire day cutting out tree overgrowth from a forest on the Mogollon Rim, a long mountain ridge across northern Arizona. They started back to their homes late in the afternoon, traveling down a pitted road in a truck driven by one of the workers. As they saw a flying craft approaching them, they at first thought it was a crashed plane hanging on the upper branches of a tall tree. It was about twenty feet in diameter and about ten feet high. As it came closer, they could not recognize it as anything terrestrial. It was a glowing flattened disk with silvery strips that divided the craft into panellike sections.

## HOW TO DEFEND YOURSELF AGAINST ALIEN ABDUCTION

All six men saw the approaching craft, but only Travis was fearless enough to jump out of the truck and walk cautiously toward it in order to get a closer look. Suddenly a bright blue beam of light emanated from the UFO and struck him; he was hurled backward onto the ground. Terrified by the inexplicable series of events, the others instantly fled the area in the truck. A little later, realizing they had left a friend in peril, some of them returned to the scene. Travis and the unidentified craft were gone.

Unknown to any of the others, he had been abducted aboard the UFO. He awakened to find himself lying on a table, with some sort of mechanical device pressing down on his chest. His vision was blurred, but he could dimly make out three figures standing around him. They were clad in orange gowns, so Travis thought that his workmates had brought him to a hospital. Suddenly, one of the figures bent over him and looked him full in the face. Travis recoiled instinctively, for the face was not human. It was, in Travis's words, "the face of a horrible creature."[5]

The creature had large luminous eyes about twice the size of human eyes. Travis realized he was in a totally alien environment, not in a hospital. All the defensive mechanisms of this young, strong Arizonan rushed to his aid. Two of the creatures were close on his right, so he instinctively struck out with his arm. He hit one of them, pushing it into the other one. Like Morgana Van Klausen, Travis realized the thin body of the one he touched was not solid or muscular, but soft, even through its clothing. The texture of the body felt spongy, "more like fat than sinew."[6] Travis quickly got off the table, feeling somewhat unsteady. As the creatures advanced, he backed away and fell against a benchful of instruments. The three entities continued to move toward him.

Revolted, Travis decided he had to avoid contact at any cost. Perhaps with the aid of a rush of adrenaline, he abruptly recovered enough to seize a cylinder-shaped device from the bench with the intent of defending himself. The cylinder was about eighteen inches long and transparent, but was too light to be used as a club. Travis tried to break the tip so that it would be sharp and more threatening. He smashed it against the metal table on which he'd been lying, but it wouldn't break.

Travis had taken years of karate. Though terrified, he sprang into a "fighting stance . . . to brace for the attack."[7] He swung out repeatedly, wielding the cylinder, shouting at the creatures to leave him alone. They slowed their advance but continued to move toward him. He cursed at them menacingly, slashing the air with the cylinder and demanding that they leave him alone. He realized he would have to dash through an open door behind them in order to escape. The creatures stopped advancing but positioned themselves between him and the door.

While he decided what to do, Travis took a good look at the creatures. Their skin had a soft, white texture, so pale they seemed translucent, as Emily Cronin's night visitors had appeared. Their garments had no buttons or zippers and did not look like human clothing. The entities were short, under five feet in stature, with very small feet. Their heads were large in proportion to their bodies, and their most prominent features were the large piercing eyes.

Travis couldn't look into their eyes because he was so repulsed; yet he found it difficult not to return his gaze repeatedly into theirs. The creatures made no sound and showed no emotion (which is typical for encounters of this kind). Travis decided he had to get out of the room but couldn't figure out how to get past the creatures without touching them. The thought of actually touching them was even more terrifying than looking at them. He made up his mind to get past them at any cost, however, but before he could put a plan into action, the three creatures suddenly turned, scurried through the door, and disappeared down a hall.

Their sudden departure gave him a chance to look for a weapon of some sort. He planned to try to escape the craft any way he could, but he needed a more substantial weapon than the thin cylinder. All of the odd-looking objects in the room were too small to be used as weapons. He threw the cylinder away and, after carefully checking to see if the creatures were returning with reinforcements, started down the curving hall.

His skirmish with the creatures seemed successful, at least for the time being. He came to a room with a single chair in it. As he entered and approached the chair, the walls and even the floor disappeared from view, and Travis looked out onto an immense scene that appeared to be outer space. He came to the conclusion that even if he did manage to escape, he could not return to Earth. He sat down in the chair and tried to work some of the mechanisms that seemed to be associated with a screenlike device in front of it. Nothing happened. After a long while, he heard a sound at the door and turned to see what looked like a human being in space clothing standing there.

Travis ran up to him. The being was tall, about six foot two, well proportioned, muscular, and weighed about two hundred pounds. Travis was so relieved to see another human being that a series of questions poured out. Where was he? How could he get out? What was going on? As he talked, he noted that the man was dressed in an unfamiliar style of helmet and clothing. The other thing that was not totally normal in his appearance were his hazel eyes. There was something odd about them, which Travis could neither understand or, later, describe. The man made no verbal response to his questions but seemed kind and willing to help. He took Travis by the arm in a nonhostile manner, and Travis willingly went with him. He was relieved because he assumed the man was a human being. He wondered why the man did not answer his questions but reasoned that the helmet prevented him from speaking.

What happened after the apparent "human being" encountered Travis and calmed his fears—giving him hope that he would be returned to Earth—is not applicable in this book. The main point in discussing the Walton case is that the witness had been able to fight off the smaller entities who had terrorized him.

As soon as Travis was relieved of his fear, however, the abduction scenario continued. He was led into the company of three other "human beings" who, although they did not wear helmets, were also completely silent and would not answer his stream of questions. These three brought about a second period of unconsciousness when Travis tried momentarily to resist them; at that point a second period of memory loss occurred. To our present knowledge, Travis still has not recovered large portions of his experience that occurred after he tried to resist the second time.

A logical question arises. Why, when Patsy Wingate clutched the neck of the small entity who had entered into her bedroom on a beam of light, was she apparently able to kill, or at least seriously disable, this creature? Patsy answers simply, "I believe in God." Similarly, why was Morgana Van Klausen able to actually touch the entity she found standing by her bedside, resulting in its immediate dematerialization and disappearance? If Wingate and Van Klausen were able to dispose of unwelcome visitors through simple Physical Struggle techniques, why didn't the creatures in the craft disappear when Travis struck out at them, pushing one of them into its companion?

We might speculate that the deeper one goes into the (unidentified) altered state that is part and parcel of almost every abduction scenario, the more "physical" the entities become. If the so-called extradimensional theory is valid, is it possible that the deeper the abductee is drawn into this dimension the more solid the entities might become? Is it possible that abducting entities, whatever or whoever they may be, are more easily "shoved" back into their own dimension while they are in the initial stages of materializing into *our* space-time?

A fourth example of a successful Physical Struggle technique was effected by a witness we will call Billy Wolfe. This case, like that of Patsy Wingate, was thoroughly investigated and documented by Don Worley and generously shared for this book. Billy Wolfe was a farmer in an isolated part of southern Illinois. His episodes of UFO encounters, which included both his father and mother, with whom he lives, began in June 1974 when Billy's father, Mitchell Wolfe, viewed a large glowing object departing from a nearby field. The next morning his son Billy, then eighteen years old, woke up and realized that his socks, which he often left on while sleeping, were dirty and damp, as if he had been walking outside without shoes. The next day he developed a bladder infection and detected a small, hard lump near his groin. He was treated for the infection, but the doctor did not seem worried about the small lump that had appeared so suddenly. It remained in place for twelve years before anything was done about it.

A neighbor of the Wolfe family had, about midnight, seen a large, lighted object descend and land in that same field. Mitchell Wolfe himself had seen a large glowing object take off from the field about 4:30 A.M. Shortly after this incident, the Wolfes moved to another house on the same farmland, but the new occupants of their former dwelling soon moved out, claiming that "ghosts" had visited both the adults and the children in their family. The ghosts were described in similar terms to the creatures known as greys.

Twelve years later, in the spring of 1986, a spot in Billy's groin near the small, hard lump began to fester. Billy was able to extract the lump. It was a thin, hard, bluish object, round, with a diameter about three-eighths of an inch. He was puzzled at its appearance, but was relieved to get rid of it. He threw it away and thought no more about it.

That same summer, the Wolfe family viewed a silver disk in the night sky that first hovered over the site of their former home (which had been demolished) and then watched, puzzled, as the object dashed toward their new home and hovered overhead. It then went straight up into the sky and disappeared. In September, they heard a loud noise that sounded as though something was pounding on their metal silo. At the same time, the security lights on their farm inexplicably went out and their shed radio ceased working. Billy Wolfe, then thirty years old, went out, armed with his rifle, to see if he could determine the cause of the interference. Seeing nothing, he returned to the house. In about fifteen minutes the lights and the radio came on again. Billy went out again, armed with his rifle, to explore what might be causing the disturbance. He happened to glance upward. To quote Don Worley's excellent report:

> Then he happened to glance up on the shed roof. There, illuminated by the light, stood a small, strange-looking figure. [Billy] stood transfixed and unbelieving. The two just stood there for a moment looking at each other. Then the figure made a slight move in [Billy's] direction. Rising fear caused [Billy] to raise his gun and take aim. Suddenly the figure was gone and he could see nothing. He took one quick shot in the darkness and ran back into the house.[8]

The appearance of the strange being on the roof triggered memories in Billy Wolfe's mind. As the days and weeks passed, bits and pieces formed into a solid memory of what had happened on that night twelve years prior when he had awakened the next morning with his socks damp and dirty. The memories were not a dream, of that Billy was sure. Instead, they were memories of something that had actually happened to him but had been long forgotten. He remembered a full abduction scenario, which had been carried out by five creatures who had large heads, big, dark eyes, and spindly bodies. They were about four and a half feet high; wore blue, tight-fitting clothing; and their skin was grayish-white. They had entered his bedroom, approaching it from the adjacent kitchen. One of them reached out and touched Billy. The touch was "just like getting a shot of Novocaine."[9] This statement implies that he was left without feeling in his body but was still able to move and walk normally.

All communication with the creatures was telepathic. They demanded that Billy come with them, and he complied. He remembered seeing the family dogs lying in the yard, as if immobilized. The creatures took him aboard an unidentified landed craft where a typical abduction scenario occurred, complete with a strange physical examination and an apparent "implanting" of the small, hard object that was removed from his groin twelve years later. Early in the scenario aboard the craft, Billy tried to resist, but was threatened with physical harm to his male organs. Understandably terrified (as any normal male would be) he stopped resisting.

The memories of the abduction were traumatizing to Billy, but he did not know what to do about them. He went on with his life as a farmer as best he could. However, the experience aboard the ship explained at least one thing that happened during the ensuing twelve years. Although a heterosexual male, he had been unable to approach women socially and therefore remained unmarried. It was a part of his life that was sorely lacking, and it greatly disturbed him.

After he realized that his 1974 abduction might have caused his inability to relate to the opposite sex and, as the Irish say, "find himself a wife," Billy was left with a deep resentment and hatred toward his abductors and toward UFO phenomena in general. By 1987, UFOs appeared around the Wolfes' farm regularly, about once a month. Starting in April 1988, they appeared even more often. They usually took the form of a reddish-orange glowing object that increased in the night sky from the size of a star to a brilliant object that was at least twice the size of the full moon. When it appeared during the day, it seemed to have an elliptical shape and shone like bright metal. It appeared in many places on the farm and surrounding areas, and sometimes came as close as two to three hundred yards.

The reappearances of the object almost invariably caused telepathic messages in Billy's head. They were sometimes derisive, at other times foreboding, but always disturbing. Billy tried to interpret them, to gain knowledge from the source, especially after he was once given the message, "Remember what we did to you!"[10] There were never any direct answers to his questions, but Billy eventually learned from the telepathic barrages that the entities who had abducted him considered him a "special project." Remembering that he had once been able to drive off one of the creatures with the threat of shooting it, he began sleeping with his gun.

On March 7, 1988, at about 10:00 P.M., Billy had the overwhelming feeling that he had to go outside; it seemed to him that the entities were demanding it. He fought valiantly against the feeling but looked out the windows of the house to see what he could detect. Through the kitchen window he saw three of the little creatures moving in a row. He quickly grabbed his rifle and stepped out the door. The beings had already vanished; perhaps they had telepathically realized he'd armed himself. He fired three shots in the direction he had seen them.

Following this incident, he experienced great relief that he had been able to drive the creatures away with the threat of firearms. He began to think that this could be a way to permanently rid himself of their harassment. Still, the family felt fear and apprehension when night fell. On May 30, at about 10:30 P.M., a thin beam of light came through the kitchen window, narrowly missing Billy, who was sitting at the table. After this, the family carefully covered all the windows in the house at night.

In August, Billy's mother awoke, hearing a scratching noise on the side of the house. Mrs. Wolfe called for help, and Billy came instantly with his gun and flashlight. He soon learned that his mother had forgotten to cover the hall window, for one of the entities was standing before it, outside the house. Billy shot at the window, and the creature disappeared from view. Since there was no dead alien body left behind, the creature either dematerialized or the bullet passed through it in a paraphysical manner—or it was fast enough to get out of the way of a speeding bullet. Unexplained mysteries like this make up the UFO phenomenon. If each tiny mystery involved could be solved, scientists could possibly find the broad answers ufologists have been seeking for fifty years.

The incessant harassment by the entities continued, and Billy's anger increased. When interviewed by Don Worley after the August 1988 incident, he had become a resentful, irate man. He told Worley, "I would love to blow their heads off!" He had decided that the entities were evil, because this was the feeling he got from them. But anger and hate have a flip side. Worley, at other times, found Billy Wolfe to be "distressed, fearful, and despondent."

"The wanton violation of one's own body leaves a profound impact on the psyche," Worley wrote. "The traumatic fallout is quite comprehensive. . . . One nearly becomes obsessed with hate and fear."[11]

As we will see in the next chapter, the technique of Righteous Anger can be effective against entity harassment, but Righteous Anger comes from a different place than the uncontrollable anger Billy Wolfe felt. However, it seemed that his intense anger, plus the use of firearms against the creatures, kept the entities at bay the majority of the time. But his embittered state disturbed his parents. They even went to the extent of having him examined by a psychiatrist, not typical for midwestern farming folk. The psychiatrist prescribed "nerve pills." This suggestion accomplished nothing for the embattled farmer and his parents.

At last contact with Worley, Billy Wolfe was still struggling with his problem, using his own unique variation of Physical Struggle to try to keep the entities at bay. Unlike Morgana Van Klausen, however, he still suspects he is being visited without his knowledge. He carefully checks his body each morning upon awakening for any telltale signs that he has been abducted during the night. The main difference between Van Klausen and Billy Wolfe is that Van Klausen used a combination of techniques with the help of an experienced researcher-counselor. She kept her emotions as even as possible, maintained self-confidence as best she could, and kept faith in the techniques she used. As a result she has been free of unpleasant visitations for several years.

Contrasted to this, Billy Wolfe's confidence in his own variation of Physical Struggle (firearms) worked well as long as his confidence in the technique lasted. When repeated visits occurred, Billy's self-confidence diminished, even though firearms caused the inquisitive entities to disappear. His confidence was replaced by intense hatred toward the entities and depression, which is essentially anger directed toward oneself. He finally lapsed into silence, writes Don Worley, after the researcher suggested other techniques to him that might help drive off what both researcher and experiencer had, by this time, decided might be truly evil beings.[12] Wolfe, in his depressed state, could not or would not follow through.

Morgana Van Klausen, Patsy Wingate, and Billy Wolfe all used their own special techniques of Physical Struggle. Morgana's was comparatively mild—a strong thought that she wanted to push the entity away, but her ability to use Physical Struggle at that point was backed up by other supportive techniques, which will be addressed when more of Morgana's resistance techniques are discussed. Patsy's successful struggle was also backed by strong faith and confidence. Billy Wolfe's was a fiercer form of Physical Struggle, which might have continued to work well if it had been backed up by self-confidence and calmer emotions.

As far as Travis Walton is concerned, his variety of Physical Struggle might *possibly* have succeeded in ending the abduction scenario if he had had knowledge of other fend-off techniques to support his initial resistance. He was convinced from the beginning of the abduction, however, that the entities and the craft on which he found himself were completely physical. This is thoroughly understandable, for six of his buddies had witnessed the initial stages of the encounter; that is, the physical craft and the ray of light that knocked him to the ground.

The Walton case is one of the few described in the UFO literature where an encounter with a UFO has been thoroughly documented and accepted by the majority of researchers. It is one of the very few that I would accept as having a high probability of being a completely physical event. However, since the six witnesses fled the scene and returned later to find Travis and the craft gone, there were no witnesses to Walton actually being taken aboard the craft. This is not to say that totally physical abductions never occur. They may occur, but not with the frequency that abductions in altered states occur.

Relating the Walton case to the subject of resistance techniques, we might speculate on the possibilities. After Travis drove away the small greys, he experienced a different scenario that led him to trust a second being whom he took to be a human being in a space suit. At that point Travis felt that he was trapped on a craft traveling through space, and therefore his original self-confidence that he could escape was gone. Meeting additional human-looking entities intensified his trust.

Is it possible that Travis Walton was deliberately deceived into believing that "human beings" were aboard the ship? Data gathered by many skilled researchers indicate that abducting entities can shape-shift. Is it therefore possible that entities can program the events in an abduction scenario in order to bring about compliance especially if a witness like Travis Walton initially resists successfully?

The cases of Billy Wolfe and Travis Walton point to the necessity of witnesses having knowledge of a *variety* of resistance techniques, because a combination of techniques is often necessary. However, each technique used must be backed up by strong self-confidence, solid belief in one's inalienable rights, and staunch faith that the resistance techniques being employed will be effective.

The Walton case, and many others that are more current, demonstrate that abductees who are caught in traumatic scenarios should not establish trust in *any* type of entity associated in any way with greys, even though they appear fully human. It has been already demonstrated in the preceding two chapters that it is possible to break abductions with which greys are connected. These creatures apparently feed on fear and are powerless against potential victims whose self-esteem and self-confidence are stronger than their own fear.

# Resistance Technique #3

---

# Righteous Anger

# RIGHTEOUS ANGER

- This technique is effective when used in initial stages of abduction and is best employed before onset of paralysis. It is also effective for paralyzed witnesses when combined with sustained Mental Struggle.

- Fearless witnesses use this technique instinctively, but less fearless witnesses can learn to use it effectively by increasing their understanding that their rights are being violated.

- Righteous Anger often builds up after repeated visitations and abductions, but the anger must be focused toward asserting one's rights rather than actual hatred directed toward the intruders.

- This technique is best combined with strong commands, either verbal or mental, such as "Go away!" "Leave me alone!" and so on.

- Even though frightened, experiencers can learn to think logically enough to put a protective plan into action, using properly focused Righteous Anger.

RIGHTEOUS ANGER IS ANOTHER RESIS-
tance technique that is often instinctively employed by witnesses. Like Mental Struggle, it is not a mysterious talent but,
rather, an ordinary ability springing from that marvelous instrument, the human mind. Righteous Anger differs from the sense
of indignation that the experiencer must feel in order for Mental
Struggle to succeed; that technique, in its simplest form, is purely
mental, while Righteous Anger surges into the realm of emotion.
It is *related* to certain aspects of anger's more intense forms—
rage, wrath, animosity, hostility, fury, and ire—but differs in significant ways. When used as a technique to drive away harassing
entities, it is a more deliberate and calmer emotion; it must be
carefully *controlled* by the experiencer if it is to be effective.
Otherwise, it can boil into the uncontrolled rage and depression
that prevented abductee Billy Wolfe from successfully ridding
himself of continued violation. It might be likened to the attitude
of the badgered news anchor in the classic movie *Network,* who
states in unequivocal terms, "I'm mad as hell, and I'm not going
to take it anymore!"

Righteous Anger is based on the solid conviction that every
human being possesses inalienable rights. Most people believe
these rights have been bestowed upon us by our Creator. They
include the right not to be violated in any way by other human
beings, or, carrying out the concept logically, any other order of
creation that might wish to harm us. In the United States, this concept is set forth in our country's founding document, the
Declaration of Independence. There it is, written for all time, that
human beings "are endowed by their Creator with certain unalien-
able rights, and that among these rights are life, liberty, and the
pursuit of happiness." Americans, then, fully understand the concept of inalienable rights. In some countries these rights are not
described in such clear terms and totalitarian regimes blatantly dis-
dain them. The majority of modern countries believe in the rights

of individual citizens, but in none are they so plainly expressed as in the United States of America.

All people, including those who live under oppressive regimes, have the concept of inalienable rights written in their hearts, even though they might not be consciously aware of this, for they are given by God, not by governments. All human beings should know that they have a right to life; all human beings should have an instinctive longing to be free of unwanted intrusion; all human beings seek happiness and, at least privately, feel entitled to it, unless these feelings have been squelched by the culture in which they live.

Provided the concept of inalienable rights is present in any particular experiencer, the link between these rights and the technique of Righteous Anger becomes clear. The main objection put forward by certain researchers is their *own certainty* that alien abductors are technologically and intellectually superior to human beings, and can therefore work their wills on their victims, in spite of the fact that many experiencers do not wish them to do so. Many researchers believe that the greys are involved in a "great plan" of human evolution, for which they have been given instructions by some vague "cosmic source." Some experiencers have come to this belief on their own, but other experiencers are influenced to believe it by the researchers. In my opinion, such witnesses are being misled.

What makes the anecdotal data even more tenuous is the fact that most of it is derived through hypnotic regression sessions. At present, there seems to be no way of scientifically verifying this theory. There is nothing in the great works of philosophy or in religious texts to indicate that humankind's spiritual or physical evolution is in the hands of creatures flying around in unidentified craft.

I believe it is appropriate to use Righteous Anger as a "fend-off" technique. In general, witnesses who are relatively fearless use it instinctively, but it can be learned by experiencers whose intrinsic personalities are less fearless. Case studies in my database indicate that this technique works best before the stage of paralysis sets in. When the next stages—of calmness and compliance— follow, the technique is no longer viable because the experiencer's mind is then rendered incapable of normal emotions.

The technique of Righteous Anger is mentioned often in my database. An excellent example occurred in the the Little Tujunga Canyon of California. It involved Jan Whitley, one of the five women discussed in *The Tujunga Canyon Contacts*.[1] Jan was a person of great willpower. She survived an unhappy childhood that included frequent physical abuse, and escaped that unwholesome environment while still in her early teens. She found a happy home with an older friend, worked part-time until she finished school, and gradually developed a solid sense of herself as a Person with Rights.

Jan had a UFO abduction experience in 1953 when she was living in an isolated cabin with a roommate, Sara Shaw (pseudonym). She and Sara were both in their early twenties. The cabin was located several miles up the mountainous road that winds from the town of Tujunga, which nestles against the foothills north of Los Angeles. At the time, Jan was working as a draftsman in an aerospace company at the foot of the mountains. One night about midnight she and Sara were awakened by light streaming into their bedroom window. Sara looked out the window, seeking the source of the unexplained light. In both witnesses' minds, there was an unspoken fear that some burly motorcyclists they had seen earlier in the evening, whizzing along the little road that ran past their cabin, had returned to make trouble for two defenseless women.

Jan moved toward her closet to get her robe, in order to help check out the light. Abruptly, time passed, about two and a half hours of forgotten memories. When Sara next looked at the clock, it read 2:20 A.M., and the light was gone. Frightened at the unexplained passage of time, the young women searched their small

cabin. Their pets, a dog and a cat, were huddled under the stove
in the kitchen; they were atypically quiet, as though frightened.
The two women fled the house, taking with them only their animals and a few items of clothing. Several days later, they conquered their fear enough to return to the cabin, accompanied by
their friend Emily Cronin.

In spite of efforts to explain the occurrence, it remained a mystery for more than twenty years. It was not until 1975, when abduction experiences began to be reported frequently, that Sara Shaw
sought advice from an investigative group that was part of the
Mutual UFO Network (MUFON) in Los Angeles, and I became
the primary investigator. In the 1970s, hypnotic regression was the
tool of choice to recover memories associated with missing time—
memories possibly linked with UFO encounters.

The full story of the 1953 encounter is covered in *The Tujunga
Canyon Contacts;* briefly stated, hypnotic-regression sessions conducted by expert hypnotherapists indicated that the two young
women were abducted aboard a Saturn-shaped craft that hovered
over a stream near their mountain cabin. Although Sara Shaw was
able to recover detailed memories of the abduction experience,
Jan Whitley was never able to recall additional memories about
this particular incident. She recalled only the fear she had felt that
night and a vague sense of intrusion by invisible presences.

According to Sara Shaw's account, the entities were about five
feet tall, thin but well proportioned, and dressed completely in
black clothing which extended over their heads and faces. They
certainly did not fit the greys' description, and Sara's experiences
aboard the craft were not particularly intrusive, compared to those
of most abductees. She did, however, recount how the group of
entities entered the cabin paraphysically through a closed window,
and how she was quickly rendered calm and compliant. She
described Jan as physically stronger than herself and offered that
as a reason why she was much more resistant toward the entities.

During Sara's retrieval of memories, she described how Jan struggled and fought with the entities as they tried to make her move out of the cabin and toward the craft hovering over the stream about fifty yards away. They did not walk in a normal fashion but "floated" above the ground, accompanied by the group of aliens. Then they were transported on a broad beam of light, which extended from the door of the craft down to the ground. By the time the aliens, with their human captives, reached the door of the craft, Jan had become limp and unresisting. The aliens had to ease her through the door, which was quite narrow in human terms. Later, aboard the craft, Sara remembered that she saw Jan physically struggling with the aliens again as they tried to remove some of her clothing.

A year after the initial missing-time experience in 1953, Jan, who was then living alone in a house in Pacoima, California, had repeated visits at night by invisible creatures, traumatizing events she consciously remembered. She always felt wide awake as the entities approached and was confident that the events were real and not dreams. The creatures had the ability to paralyze her, but they could not control her mind; by that time, she had developed into a person with great willpower and considerable metaphysical knowledge. Jan felt Righteous Anger instinctively toward the intruders; she believed they were invading her territory and trespassing on what she considered her inalienable rights.[2]

In a hypnotic-regression session in the 1970s conducted by Dr. Bill McCall, Jan described the incessant assaults of the invisible presences:

> JAN: There were only mental push-and-pull situations, which were very disturbing, and very frightening, until I got angry and told them to go away. And they did.
> McCALL: *What* did you tell to go away?
> JAN: No shape, no forms, no nothing. It was just a mental contest, that's the only way I can think to call it.

McCALL: Who is *they?*

JAN: I don't know. I never even thought that—but it seemed like a whole bunch. I never thought of it being just individual. I always thought of it collectively as "they."[3]

By describing the experiences as "mental push-pull situations," Jan was trying to put a label on what happened during these recurring episodes. The invisible entities came to her every night for months, and each time Jan heard a high, piercing sound, akin to that heard by Emily Cronin. The invisible visitors invariably insisted that Jan "come with them" (where and why was never explained.) The intrusive, loud noise seemed to be a way of enforcing their demands, and Jan invariably resisted "going with them." She considered it an intrusion on her privacy *and* her right to make her own decisions. She had another even more sagacious reason for resisting: she always definitely felt that "they" never intended to bring her back. She instinctively used mental struggle against them at first, willing them to go away. The technique apparently worked, for when she could feel them going away, her paralysis broke, and she was able to sleep peacefully through the night.

The attacks continued nightly, however, and Jan finally got fed up with them. She began to scream mentally at the invisible intruders, telling them to "Go away and leave me alone!" When she reached this stage of resistance, which I call Righteous Anger, the episodes abruptly stopped. Righteous Anger worked faster for Jan than Mental Struggle and was lasting. The final attack occurred after she moved into another house in the Tujunga Canyons, where she lived alone. This time she saw the creatures as distorted faces hovering around her bed. She screamed at them, ordering them to "Go away!" After that, she was free of them for the rest of her life.

In April 1979, during a later interview, Jan revealed that she felt something was trying "to take my mind from my body" during these experiences and always intuitively felt that if she gave in "something terrible" would happen to her. She invariably insisted that these experiences were not dreams and that she was awake when they occurred. This, in spite of Dr. McCall's repeated attempts to explain to her that many people, including himself, had similar experiences at times, and that they were some kind of nightmare or vivid dream.

Since the 1970s investigation of the Whitley case, many experienced psychotherapists and psychiatrists in the UFO field have come to the same conclusion that Jan and other experiencers affirm—that these types of experiences are not normal dreams in any sense of the word, but probably occur in an as-yet-unidentified altered state that constitutes essentially an "altered reality." Jan's experiences were "real" to her, but they may not have taken place totally in our normal space-time reality. However, her fear and terror—and consequently the sense of Righteous Anger that Jan was able to produce in herself and project toward the entities—were also real.

In spite of attempts by three experienced hypnotists, Jan was never able to recall any visual details of the 1953 abduction scenario that she shared with Sara Shaw. At first, it was suspected that Jan was one of those rare persons who cannot be hypnotized. As the investigation progressed over a period of four years, it became apparent that she slipped into a light to moderate trance each time she was hypnotized but was not retrieving any "meaningful" details—meaning that she could not retrieve details similar to what other abductees were able to recall. Instead, she recalled colors, mainly purple, and vivid feelings of terror and anger.

The fact that Sara Shaw and Emily Cronin had been able to retrieve rich details of their experiences intrigued Jan, and she had a vigorous curiosity about it. Even though she was not an easily hypnotized subject, certain post-hypnotic suggestions given during the first and second attempts did bring forth memories of the experience in the cabin with Sara. She was able to recall, consciously, that she had become inexplicably immobilized while she was walking toward her closet to get her robe. Her descriptions, given in a February 1979 interview, are revealing because they are so vivid and add much to what she had been unable to describe in prior sessions:

> I remembered being frightened, but it was more than fear. The pain was the worst. Physical pain, a terrible headache, and I never get headaches. It was like somebody had a steel band on there, just *crunching* it and pressing it down. It also seemed as if all the oxygen had been taken out of the air.

At this point Jan stopped, groping for the right words to describe something totally foreign to her experience. Although normally articulate, she had difficulty describing what she now remembered. She finally summarized it: "The best way I can describe it is that the atmospheric pressure changed."[4]

This statement was significant, for Jan deliberately resisted reading anything about UFOs. Even after their missing-time experience had been under intensive investigation for several years, Jan avoided books and articles on UFOs. She never even read the book that had been written about her own experiences and those of her friends. Sara Shaw had described the atmosphere around the cabin as extremely quiet, as if a vacuum had been placed around it. During many close encounters, particularly those involving abducting creatures, witnesses report that the atmosphere around their home or vehicle changes. Some describe it as "like being in a vacuum," others remark that normal outdoor noises, which are part and parcel of their environment, are either muted or absent altogether. The 1979 interview indicated that Jan was beginning to retrieve at least a little of her lost memory.

Eventually, in a particularly relaxed hypnotic session, she was able to describe in rather unique terms what she felt was the basic nature of the "creatures" or "intelligences" involved in her terrifying experiences. She stated with absolute certainty that, in all of her experiences with them, the creatures were "invisible" but at the same time "absolutely real." Furthermore, she stated that she was never able to discern anything about what their ultimate purposes or motives might be.

We might be able to learn something from this stolid, honest person about the basic nature of abduction scenarios and gain a valuable clue about the fundamental nature of abducting entities. In later chapters we will delve further into the theory that "invisible but entirely real" entities reportedly have been harassing and abducting human beings for thousands of years.

Righteous Anger as a resistance technique is more commonly used than the UFO literature reveals. It has been described in an almost offhand fashion, as if the act of driving off an intrusive entity is just one more detail in an otherwise typical abduction case. An example is the following case investigated by the MUFON Pensacola Chapter. The incident occurred in Pensacola, Florida, in April 1987, and the primary investigator was Joe Barron.

About 2:00 A.M., the woman witness (who desires anonymity) awoke and saw a brilliant light in the bedroom that had not been there before. She then saw a typical grey in a column of white light, which was coming down from the ceiling. The creature was about three and a half feet tall and was floating close to the ceiling, within a rainbow of colors encased within the white light beam. The woman witness was, at the time, sixty-seven years old and retired. However, her personality was anything but retiring. She is described in Joe Barron's investigative report as "a competent person . . . handles her own affairs, owns her home, a car, and keeps close contact with her friends, neighbors, and in particular her family. They appear to be a close-knit family and supportive of one another. In my opinion, she is cooperative and has given sound and accurate testimony.[5]

The woman was naturally frightened at the sight of the creature. But she was also angry, as she explained to Barron, because the entity had the nerve to come into her bedroom and invade her privacy. Instead of lapsing into terrorized silence she made an exclamation of surprise, jumped out of bed, and turned on the light. The creature and the column of light to which it clung remained in full view, and the witness had ample time to observe all details of its physical features and clothing. The two stared at each other, only about three feet separating them. No communication, telepathic or verbal, passed between them.

The woman thought about fleeing through the nearby bedroom door, but instinctively felt that the column of light would somehow "get" her. She noted that everything seemed abnormally quiet. Finally the witness, in spite of her continuing fear, yelled at the creature, "Get outa here!" Immediately, the column of light seemed to "bubble" with colors. The entity climbed toward the ceiling "as if climbing a ladder," looking at her all the time it was climbing. When it reached the top, it disappeared through the ceiling, and the beam of light vanished with it.[6]

The witness experienced no immediate aftereffects. Instead, she left the bedroom, got a hammer and screwdriver from the kitchen, and inspected the ceiling and windows, looking for possible entry marks that would explain to her, logically, how the creature came through the ceiling. She could find none. In order to assure herself that she did not dream or otherwise invent the experience, she placed the hammer and screwdriver on her dresser so that she could see if they were there in the morning. They were.

The witness emphasized to investigator Joe Barron that she was fully awake, and that the experience was real and not a dream.

She suffered physical aftereffects of the encounter in the form of black blotches on her skin with some bumps that could not be diagnosed. She also experienced swelling of her eyes, which became painful and bulging. After consulting two doctors, a medication was prescribed that cleared up her skin within two weeks. The curious and otherwise unexplained physical effects only serve to strengthen the witness's statements that something real had, indeed, occurred.

This witness, like Jan Whitley, successfully used the technique of Righteous Anger in fending off the imminent approach of an intruding, unidentified entity. As in Jan's case, the Pensacola witness instinctively used the technique. Her anger was accompanied by a feeling that her privacy had been invaded; therefore it is clear that she, like Jan, had a sense of her own rights. Righteous Anger is often used instinctively by relatively fearless individuals who, although experiencing normal (and often lifesaving) fear, can nevertheless continue to think calmly and logically and put a protective plan into action. Righteous Anger, like the other resistance techniques previously described, can be learned by persons who are willing to make the effort. It must be emphasized that Righteous Anger must occur before paralysis sets in, for the sense of paralysis (whether it is so-called paralyzing fear or an actual physiological condition) often leads to the next steps—a sense of calmness that leads to compliance to the entities' instructions. However, as in Jan Whitley's case, the fact that the woman "felt paralyzed" did not prevent her from screaming at the entity and demanding that it "leave her alone!"

For Righteous Anger to work best, therefore, witnesses need to be *relatively* fearless with a firm sense of their own rights. This technique is surprisingly similar to one that law enforcement officers teach in citizen safety classes. When faced by a common street criminal, who typically doesn't carry a gun—such as a purse snatcher or mugger—citizens are advised to yell audible protests instead of merely screaming out of fear and terror. Screaming, even for the precise intention of obtaining help in a dangerous situation, is essentially an *unfocused* action. It startles people who are within earshot and makes them afraid to offer help. All too rarely does screaming alert people who are fearless enough to defend the rights of a stranger.

In citizen safety classes conducted by police officers in many large cities where crime is rampant, citizens are specifically advised to respond to unarmed street criminals with loud commands like, "Go away!" or "You haven't any right!" The unexpected fearless stance of the potential victim usually throws an unarmed criminal off guard, and he might simply flee the scene, aware that this particular individual isn't going to be an easy target. If the street criminal does *not* flee, the loud, assertive voice of the potential victim often informs people within earshot that someone's rights are being violated, and they become *curious* instead of fearful. They draw closer to the action, perhaps in groups, and it is not uncommon to have more than one irate citizen experiencing Righteous Anger, fearlessly pursuing the criminal, and actually apprehending him.

It is well for witnesses using Righteous Anger as a resistance technique to remember that even though the entities might seem extraterrestrial in nature and more technologically advanced, there are indications in the UFO literature that these creatures can shape-shift at will, assuming any form they wish.[7] This aspect will be covered at more length in the last chapter, where other types of abducting entities, reported in many world cultures down through the millennia, are addressed.

It is possible that the public image of the abducting greys is horrifying enough that many people when confronted will simply comply with their instructions to come with them. Growing evidence exists, however, substantiating the theory that the initial materialization of intrusive entities is accomplished while the witness is in a light altered state, such as the slight trance a person experiences while driving, watching television, or awakening from sleep. This light trance can be easily broken by human beings when they sense the approach of abductors and Righteous Anger, in particular, breaks through the altered state in its *initial stages*. Entities who are allegedly responsible for abductions seem to depend on altered states to render the witness compliant.

It is important for witnesses who wish to learn how to use Righteous Anger to realize that this particular technique must be used in the initial stages of abduction. Typically, this requires four elements:

1. The potential victims are awake, or at least *think* that they are awake.
2. They are capable of moving their bodies sufficiently to take a threatening stance or, at the very least, utter threatening verbal demands.
3. They have either an instinctive or acquired strong sense of their own rights to privacy and freedom from unwanted intrusion.
4. They have enough self-esteem—either natural or trained—so that Righteous Anger bubbles to the surface easily when these rights are jeopardized.

Another example of Righteous Anger comes from Rev. Harrison E. Bailey, a Baptist minister who lives in Pasadena, California. His experience with UFO entities began in 1951 when he was verbally accosted in broad daylight by two occupants in a landed UFO. At the time, he was a steelworker in Gary, Indiana, and was on vacation, walking at midday through a patch of wooded land outside Orland Park, Illinois. Two masked entities appeared at the door of the UFO and asked him questions. He remembered answering them briefly and then continued on his way.

*A 1978 sketch by UFO colleague "SCM" depicting Harrison E. Bailey's encounter with a landed UFO in an Illinois wooded area, on September 24, 1951.*

Shortly after the encounter Bailey felt deeply fatigued, even though he was a strong, athletic young man. Added to the inexplicable fatigue, he was afflicted with painful, cramping sensations in his shoulders, arms, legs, and abdomen. Four or five hours seemed to have passed inexplicably, for the sun was now low in the west. When he reached the next town, he encountered a crowd of people who were talking excitedly about seeing a "flying saucer." They asked him if he knew anything about it, but this was before the days of the civil rights struggle and, being black, Bailey realized he might jeopardize his steelworking job if he spoke out openly about the UFO he'd seen.[8]

Harrison Bailey never recovered his former strength and vigor. He had gallbladder surgery in 1963 and while at the hospital experienced two vivid "dreams," during which he felt he had been taken aboard a UFO similar to the one he'd encountered in 1951. Aboard the UFO, he spoke to two occupants whose appearance was also similar. A "message" was imparted to him; mainly, that he should alert the American people and the federal government that UFOs were real, had benevolent motives, and that they wished to land and communicate with humans but were hesitant to do so for fear of being harmed.

Bailey argued with the occupants, telling them that scientists or high government officials would be the logical people to contact—influential people who could reach out to the whole of American society and whose words would be heeded. In 1963, Bailey was still employed at the steel mill and could not speak out for fear of losing his job. He could not accept these two experiences as mere dreams, however. They were so real that he asked the nurses if he'd been missing from his hospital room, but their replies were noncommittal.

The dreams were so vivid, however, that he suspected they could possibly be real encounters, perhaps experienced in some kind of altered reality. Eventually, he retired from the steel mills in 1966 on a disability pension and soon afterward began to speak out about his 1951 encounter, his subsequent dreams, and the entities' message to the American people. From 1966 to 1975 he did everything he could to alert the public and various government officials that "flying saucers" were real and wished to land.

He met mostly ridicule and discouragement from friends and strangers alike and was the subject of occasional human interest articles in newspapers that treated his report with sardonic humor. Some of the government officials he wrote to answered his letters, but with indifference. Still he persisted. He decided to become a minister, was educated at a ministerial college in Gary, and moved to the West Coast to take up pastoral work in Baptist churches in Pasadena.

By now he had become convinced that his decline in health resulted directly from some type of emission, perhaps radiation, from the UFO. He has distinct memories of being informed by his doctors after his 1963 gallbladder surgery that his internal organs were "considerably more aged" than his chronological age would indicate. Bailey neither smoked nor drank, did not abuse drugs, nor did he engage in any other activity that would accelerate aging of his body.[9]

When speaking out publicly about his UFO experiences and the entities' message, he mentioned the advanced aging of his organs, terming it "flying saucer disease." He often asked his listeners if they knew of any other cases where similar physiological damage had been noted after a close encounter with a UFO. After nine years, he finally came to the attention of experienced UFO researchers, who set about trying to document his claims.

Although Rev. Bailey is a good-natured, intelligent, and patient human being, he was inwardly distressed that the entities had charged him with the responsibility of alerting the public. As his efforts to spread the message through newspaper ads, flyers, and occasional public appearances were repeatedly ignored, he developed mild Righteous Anger toward the entities. He kept it under control for years, but it was always in his mind. Even in our initial interview, he expressed annoyance that the UFO beings had not chosen scientists or government officials to spread the word.

I first met Rev. Bailey in 1975 when he appeared on a television talk show in Los Angeles. A lengthy investigation of his case began, which is still ongoing. In one of our first interviews, with the aid of a map, he described his walk from the forest near Orland Park, Illinois, to a small railroad town where he spent the night. It became apparent that a period of missing time had occurred. He had always wondered about the discrepancy but had no idea what it could possibly mean.

In 1975, hypnotic regression was used routinely on emotionally sound individuals to recover missing-time memories associated with UFO close encounters. With the help of Bert Schwarz, M.D., a psychiatrist who is also a parapsychologist and noted UFO researcher, Bailey underwent personality testing in the Los Angeles area by a qualified psychotherapist referred by Schwarz. He tested essentially normal, except for a slight paranoid tendency, which is typical of most abductees. This slight tendency is accepted as normal for these individuals, because the majority of them have sustained years of ridicule and sarcasm from friends and strangers alike.

Bailey was hypnotically regressed by Dr. Bill McCall. He proved to be a good hypnosis subject, easily recovering peripheral memories of the 1951 event, which had been wiped from his conscious memory. He experienced considerable difficulty, however, in describing details of an apparent actual abduction scenario *aboard* the UFO. When he reached this block, he explained to Dr. McCall, "Even if something like that had happened to me, I wouldn't want to admit it, being a black man in a white society." Upon being reassured that this was the late 1970s, not 1951, and that no harm would come to him as a result, Bailey, under hypnosis, gave details of boarding the UFO by means of a ramp that extended from the craft. The entities conducted a cursory examination, directed mainly at his head and facial features.

The entities were about five feet in height and seemed benevolent enough, but Bailey avoided looking at them too closely. They wore green-tinted "shields," which reminded him of the face shields worn by steelworkers at the blast furnaces. Behind these shields, their faces looked grotesquely flattened, as if the transparent material distorted their features. The entities gave him a message to tell the American people that UFOs were real, that they meant no harm, and that they desired to land unhindered. The demand was delivered telepathically in unaccented English. It was the same message he consciously remembered hearing during his later 1963 experiences. Bailey balked at their demand, for at the time he was an ordinary working man and knew his words would carry little weight.

He was eventually released by the entities and walked down the ramp to the road. As he walked away, all memory of being inside the UFO slipped from his mind, but he retained conscious memories of seeing the landed craft and the two strange "men" who had looked out at him through a window. He was also left with a persistent urge to read about UFOs and find out everything he could about them. He had been unable to understand fully this strong urge until after he was regressed by Dr. McCall on September 28, 1977.

In spite of the fact that Bailey tried actively for years to pass on the entities' message he achieved only minimal success. He believed he'd been given an almost impossible task but initially controlled his irritation. His annoyance grew stronger as a series of events started in the late 1970s.

Around 1978, his slim finances were in severe jeopardy. His position as assistant pastor at the Pasadena Baptist church gave him little fiscal remuneration, and his disability pension had been abruptly cut off. As a result of these problems, Rev. Bailey experienced severe stress. While managing to maintain an equitable, good-natured approach toward his ministerial duties, he began to sleepwalk at night—a sign of subconscious turmoil. Rev. Bailey had always been a vigorous walker, especially during his younger days, and even after his surgery and during his years of pastoral work he walked daily for exercise. But now he began sleepwalking late at night through the streets of Pasadena and into adjacent cities. Kindly police more than once found him and brought him home. Besides the sleepwalking, he began to experience frequent entity visits. These invariably happened in the middle of the night; sometimes they occurred in conjunction with his sleepwalking and sometimes they occurred while he was sleeping in bed.

These entity visits seemed somewhat like vivid dreams, but Rev. Bailey suspected they might be real. It seemed as though the entities were growing impatient that he had not yet succeeded in carrying out their demands to alert the American public. The visits were more frequent than before, occurring as often as once a week for several months. Sometimes the creatures were fully materialized when he first became aware of them, and sometimes they materialized before his eyes. Their appearance was somewhat different from the entities he remembered seeing in the landed UFO. They did not have the distinct masks, and were somewhat shorter. But they invariably demanded, "Why aren't you getting out our message?"

Bailey's patience grew thin. He now resented the incessant intrusion. What bothered him, perhaps most of all, was his inability to determine if these dreams were real or, perhaps, merely a side effect of the medication his doctor had prescribed for sleepwalking. On my advice Rev. Bailey bought an inexpensive Polaroid One-Step camera and kept it by his bedside. The idea was this: If he could succeed in photographing the entities, the photos would indicate that they were physically real and not simply his imagination or dreams. If he succeeded in getting photos—physical proof that the entities were real—the pictures could be presented to scientists. This would satisfy a major part of the entities' message, and they might cease their incessant demands.

A few months passed. Then, early in the morning of November 1, 1978, the entities returned. Bailey was asleep. He had intended to go with a friend to a Halloween party at his church that evening but, feeling somewhat unwell, decided against it. He had purchased two plastic Halloween masks for the occasion, but since he'd not had a chance to use them he'd placed them on a table near his bed. He awakened suddenly about 1:40 A.M. and saw two of the entities in his apartment. Only their heads had materialized, brown, bald, three-dimensional, with only a suggestion of shoulders underneath. They stood out distinctly against his beige window shades and were illuminated by the glow of a 40-watt lightbulb Bailey habitually kept burning all night in the adjacent bathroom.

Not quite sure what to make of the situation, Bailey got out of bed and turned on other lights in his studio apartment. His eyes burned, and his head throbbed. He washed his face, hoping he was merely dreaming. When he returned to bed, the faces were still at the window, waiting. They spoke to him, repeating their demand that he spread the word about UFOs.

"Look," Bailey replied, righteously annoyed, "I've got troubles of my own, and I don't think I'm the right person for this job. Why don't you go ask somebody with some influence to help you?"

"Your financial problems will be settled soon," the heads replied.

The conversation continued in the same tiresome terms. Bailey suddenly remembered his camera, and asked the entities if he could take their pictures, telling them that photos would provide proof he could present to scientists. The full story of how Bailey took pictures of the entities and the strange metamorphoses the entities apparently performed are described in various journals, articles, newspaper accounts, and books in the UFO literature.[10] One of the photos, considered the best Bailey obtained that night in an unprecedented series of UFO entity photos, appeared in a technical journal, *IEEE Aerospace and Electronic Systems*.[11]

The importance of the Bailey case to our subject of resistance techniques is that he eventually reacted against them with a form of Righteous Anger and as a direct result succeeded in ridding himself of the intrusive visits.

Significantly, after a second photo session, Rev. Bailey was never again harassed by unidentified intruders. This suggests that his mild form of Righteous Anger resulted in ending the entities' visits. His November 1, 1978, series of photos have attracted continuing study by unbiased experts, the latest of which is a skillful scientist with state-of-the-art computer enhancement equipment. Some rather surprising results were achieved (see the last chapter).

We might theorize from the cases reported above that various degrees of Righteous Anger can fend off harassing bedroom visitors. Some of the successful experiencers were prone to normal levels of human anger and were able to focus it against the intruders in such a way that their emotions did not get in the way of their sustained self-esteem and their unshakable conviction that their rights were being violated. In other words, normal levels of Righteous Anger were focused to a point of convergence, which was directed *toward the entities,* instead of being diffused. Rev. Bailey's "anger" was never strong, but his increasing annoyance was nevertheless well focused—and so, we might say, was his camera!

Focusing Righteous Anger toward the source of the anger makes it effective. Diffused anger is *never* effective as a resistance technique. Harassed abductees who wish to end the intrusion into their lives would do well to study the difference between focused Righteous Anger and diffused, desperate anger, especially since many high-profile abduction researchers contend that anger toward entities never prevents abduction scenarios. Understanding the difference between focused Righteous Anger, which comes from a place of confidence in one's inalienable rights, and diffused anger, which comes from negative emotions such as despair and depression, could make many abductees' lives more enjoyable and uncomplicated.

# Resistance Technique #4

---

# Protective Rage

# PROTECTIVE RAGE

- The main intent of this technique is to protect other members of the household, especially small children and others unable to protect themselves.

- The technique is best employed before paralysis sets in, since it involves the human voice used strongly and assertively, using rejecting statements, even well-chosen curses, hurled toward the intruders.

- Protective Rage must be focused toward the intruders who are violating your rights. Like Righteous Anger it must not be rooted in fear and despair from which negative results spring. Uncontrolled anger is *never* effective.

- The term "Protective Rage" might seem contradictory, but it is in its illogic that its effectiveness is rooted. Rage in this context means ardor, which encompasses fidelity, love, and loyalty, all of which are devoid of negative aspects.

- Protective Rage is combined with a wish that the intruders not be harmed, only told to cease their visits and leave your family alone. Hold no grudge or hatred after the fact.

- The technique can be used at the time of the visitations or afterward. When used after the entities depart, it is best combined with other techniques to ensure lasting results.

**A**NOTHER FEND-OFF TECHNIQUE, WHICH I call Protective Rage, is akin to Righteous Anger but involves even stronger emotions. Like Righteous Anger and Physical Struggle it is best employed *before* paralysis sets in, since it involves speaking strongly and assertively. Unlike the four techniques discussed thus far, it is effective even *after* an abduction in helping to prevent future visits. Unlike Righteous Anger, which needs only a few well-chosen, assertive phrases, Protective Rage involves repeated verbal rejection of the entities.

The aspect that separates this technique from the others is that it protects others in the experiencer's family who are being harassed by the abductors. This particularly applies to an experiencer's children, for the guilt a parent feels being unable to protect them is perhaps the most destructive emotion an abductee undergoes.

Those witnesses who have an urgent need to protect family members are well advised to try Protective Rage when they first realize that abduction scenarios are being experienced by anyone in the family. It sometimes takes years of such encounters before any family member tells another that they are being harassed. This is one of the least understood aspects of alien abduction, but it was discovered by several researchers independently and is now generally accepted as part and parcel of the abduction phenomenon.

In employing the technique of Protective Rage, violent language is hurled against the intruders. Well-chosen curses can be used if the experiencer is acquainted with any. Most cultures have maledictions rooted in their language and tradition. The Irish, for example, have rather charming curses that are not only effective but humorous. Humor is an integral part of the long history of the Irish and resulted, at least in part, from their efforts to survive seven centuries of oppression. Instead of becoming embittered, the Irish used humor to survive ethnically intact. But Irish humor is carefully focused in its focused *illogic*—as is the resistance technique of Protective Rage.

Protective Rage must first of all be focused. Like Righteous Anger it must not be rooted in fear and despair, from which negative results spring. It is best used by assertive persons who have faith that the technique will be effective. If their self-confidence in the technique does not originate from personal experience, they should at least have assurances from sources they respect that it has been effective for others. If witnesses who wish to try this technique are not naturally assertive or relatively fearless, the technique can still work if the witnesses decide it is worthwhile to give it a try. Sometimes counseling by researchers or therapists who have faith in the technique can help install in the witnesses the fortitude to try it.

Protective Rage has been used successfully by several witnesses in my database of resisters, and has been known to bring about the rapid departure of intrusive entities. An outstanding example of its success is found in the case of Morgana Van Klausen, whose encounters with white-skinned bedroom visitors were described in Technique #2. Protective Rage employs vocalization of strong, rejecting language, intended to protect other members of the household as well as oneself. It was the last of a series of techniques used by Morgana, all of which combined to bring about eventual success.

The Van Klausen family visitations began in December 1986 and continued through May 1991. During this time, Morgana experienced monthly disturbing occurrences. As upsetting as her personal experiences were, even more disturbing was the fact that her young son, who was four years old in 1987, repeatedly told her that "clowns" came through the walls of his bedroom at night. He also called these visitors "ghosts." Morgana carefully refrained from telling him anything about her own frightening experiences, but now she feared that her child was also being visited by unidentified entities. One morning her son, who is intelligent and advanced beyond his years in certain skills, made a drawing of an aircraft-type vehicle with "people" aboard it. He insisted that he had traveled on the "airplane" the previous night.

He also drew pictures of airplanes on which he had taken trips with his parents and reminded his mother about these excursions, which he remembered well. Then he pointed out the differences in his drawing between the airplanes on which he had traveled in the company of his parents and the "airplane" on which he had been the previous night. Even allowing for deficiencies in the drawing skills of a four-year-old, his sketch shows distinct differences between the two kinds of aircraft.

Morgana was outraged when she realized that her son was being actively harassed, perhaps even abducted, by the "people" or "ghosts" he had told her about. She felt intense anger, along with maternal guilt that she had been unable to prevent these occurrences. This mixture of anger and guilt gave her the strength to decide to resist the creatures and eventually resulted in the "pushing" incident, described in Technique #2, by which she was able to cause an entity to vanish through Physical Struggle.

Aware that I was actively studying case histories of abductees who had been able to fend off their abductors, Morgana sought my advice on how best to go about it. She was the first experiencer in the Los Angeles area to seek my help with resistance. All the others in my growing database up till then had either instinctively fended off their harassers or had sought help from family members.

One of Morgana's main problems was her husband's initial indifferent attitude toward her experiences. To his knowledge he had not been bothered by the creatures and, being a practical, science-trained professional, decided that the episodes being described by his wife and son were either vivid dreams or imagination. Since his work took him away at night many times a month for late meetings with clients and professional groups, he was not at home during many of the UFO events.

One night in May 1988, however, Morgana's husband, whom we shall call Luke, awoke to see what he later termed "two people" standing in the hall outside their bedroom. He felt totally paralyzed, unable to move to a nearby drawer to get his handgun, which he kept for home defense. He tried frantically to tell Morgana to "get the gun," but this time it was Morgana who slept peacefully through the event. This single experience changed Luke's attitude. He discussed it with her the following morning, expressing his bewilderment over what had happened. He especially wondered who the "people" were and why she hadn't awakened when he called out for help.

Even more important, Luke became much more supportive of Morgana and the fact that she was reporting ongoing experiences with UFO-type phenomena. He no longer argued with her and actually helped her install and put into use protective devices in the home. At about the same time, Morgana discussed the happenings with investigators and was now convinced that the episodes that had occurred in her family home were real events. Any suspicion she might have held that they might have been dreams or imagination ceased, and she was determined to get rid of the phenomena once and for all. She developed a lot of anger against the repeated visits, for they were upsetting her home life and keeping her nerves on edge.

Morgana developed her own process of Protective Rage after she acquired the fortitude to believe she could keep the entities away. She accidentally discovered that leaving the hall light on all night kept the entities away from both her son's bedroom and the bedroom she shared with her husband. Each morning, she opened all the curtains and windows in her large house, allowing the bright California sun and fresh air to fill it. Together with this, she began to talk out loud to the entities, focusing her words toward them. She would stand in the living room, direct her Protective Rage toward the (now invisible) entities and verbally repeat phrases such as "Keep out of my house!" and "You are not wanted here!" She fervently "explained" that they were not to come back because they were causing trouble for her family and for herself.

Morgana repeatedly sent these messages to the entities over a period of days. Although they were not around in any sense that she could detect, she suspected that they might be able to hear her in some unknown manner. She did not know for sure, of course, but she still felt she was helping to protect her family by this technique. Her success can be measured by the indisputable fact that the visits by the entities ceased.

The very notion of deliberately focusing Protective Rage against entities who are not even visible (or perhaps not even "there" in any logical sense of the word) might seem absurd to some readers. However, the scale by which any resistance technique should be measured is success.

Although *rage* can mean fury, madness, and raving, the technique of Protective Rage holds none of these connotations. Rage in its more positive aspects can mean ardor, fervor, and zeal. These definitions describe the rage used by Morgana Van Klausen and other experiencers who rid their homes and families of unwelcome abductors. In fact, the most accurate description is ardor. Ardor encompasses the positive qualities of fidelity, love, loyalty, and devotion.

Morgana Van Klausen's motivation in using Protective Rage against the harassing entities was to defend her family—not only her small son who was possibly experiencing full abduction-scenarios, but also her husband. Morgana, in focusing Protective Rage against entities who were violating her family's inalienable rights was expressing love, loyalty, and devotion toward her son and husband. She focused her efforts successfully against the creatures who were depriving her family of these protective virtues. She was taking back her rights—no more, no less. After five full years of living under stress and uncertainty, she was able to resume a normal life and has now been free of bedroom encounters for seven years. It isn't known just how the technique of Protective Rage works, especially when used after the fact. We can, however, offer a speculation. Perhaps the self-confidence and self-esteem of the person using it builds a psychic shield over the home. Perhaps the entities, whoever they are and whatever their true source, can actually sense the rejection being hurled at them, even when they are not physically present. The technique might even be related in some way to the process of exorcism by which trained ministers, priests, and spiritually minded psychics can cause unwholesome entities, who are apparently "possessing" human beings, to depart. This is not to say that so-called abducting aliens are akin to those orders of creation called devils, or demons—terms that equate in the Judeo-Christian tradition with fallen angels—although the parallels are most interesting and should be explored further by qualified researchers in ufology and religion.[1]

It is interesting to note, however, that it could be said that Jesus used a form of Protective Rage when he overturned the money-changers' tables at the Temple in Jerusalem. His intent was not to harm the money-changers, and he did not hate them. However, he did realize that he had to take forceful verbal and even physical action to protect the Temple from noxious influences. We will explore how to invoke the Protective Rage of spiritual guardians in the chapter on Appeal to Spiritual Personages.

The proof that positive motives work in successful resistance lies in the experiences of several resisters discussed in this book. Morgana Van Klausen has resumed her life with no resentments toward the prior intruders. Other former experiencers like Emily Cronin and Melissa MacLeod hold no grudge against the entities who have traumatized them. They consider them as part of the whole of life. As Emily Cronin states eloquently, "All life is one."

Summarizing the technique of Protective Rage, it works best when assertive witnesses have an urgent need to protect their families. It can be used during and *after* an abduction to prevent future visits. Violent language and even well-chosen curses can be used, but the rage must be carefully focused in an attitude of inviolable rights, self-esteem and confidence in one's self, and in the efficacy of the techniques. Uncontrolled anger rooted in fear and despair is *never* effective.

It isn't known just how this technique works when utilized after the fact. We might speculate that it provides a psychic shield over the home or that the entities are able to sense the added rejection being hurled at them. We would have to know more about the true nature of abducting entities in order to explain this. The main point to be emphasized, when speaking of both Righteous Anger and the stronger technique, Protective Rage, is that the experiencers should hold no grudge or hatred after the fact.

# Resistance
# Technique
# #5

---

# Support
# from
# Family
# Members

## SUPPORT FROM FAMILY MEMBERS

- By "family" we mean not only blood relatives the witness lives with or sees often, but also close friends.

- The old adage "two heads are better than one" applies here. Members of an experiencer's family may already be acquainted with the phenomenon of harassing entities and found ways to fend them off that they can share. The abduction phenomenon is generational in nature.

- Support from Family Members must be directed toward solving the problem of the *visitations*, not directed toward "curing" the experiencer's emotional trauma by consulting therapists who have no knowledge of bedroom visitors.

- Family support is best used in combination with other resistance techniques, especially when other family members are experiencing the same type of harassment.

- Family support is used naturally in close-knit cultures where harassing entities are recognized in religious and societal beliefs and not just as folklore.

- Re-recognition of Old World information and faith in the family members offering it is necessary for successful results.

ANOTHER POWERFUL TECHNIQUE FOR resisting abducting bedroom visitors can be called Support from Family Members. By "family" I mean not only blood relatives the witness lives with or sees often, but also close friends with whom they share confidences. In normal everyday life, small children assume that their parents can, and will, protect them from harm. A common phrase used by small boys, especially, when harassed by other boys at school is to say firmly, "My daddy can beat your daddy!" The simple sentence carries implications that the child feels protected by his father, and knows that this protection gives him the courage to confront other kids who might want to hurt him. Just as Protective Rage is activated when those close to us are threatened, feeling support by our loved ones protects us.

The natural reluctance on the part of many witnesses to ask support from family and friends is completely understandable, but because the abduction phenomenon is so widespread, we encourage witnesses to do it. Several vivid examples of the successful use of this powerful technique may give additional ideas to experiencers who have tried to seek help from family members, but, failing initially, made no more attempts to tap this source.

Morgana Van Klausen, whose years-long siege has been described, found great comfort and help when her husband, Luke, finally started supporting her. Although initially he did not believe Morgana was experiencing real occurrences, he eventually began to develop ideas that he thought might help his wife with her growing stress. Morgana had mentioned to Luke that she believed leaving on the lights and ceiling fan helped deter the nighttime visitors. To her surprise, Luke began to turn on the lights in the hall himself when they went to bed.

On his own volition, Luke also bought ceiling fans for every room in the house and installed them himself. This was an unprecedented action for this practical, science professional. Although he had discussed his one experience with the bedroom visitors with her the morning after it occurred, he never again mentioned it. It was as if he wanted to block the experience from his mind. His protective and supportive action of installing the ceiling fans and his cooperation in leaving the lights on at night were, however, extremely supportive to her. She began to feel much less stress, not only because the creatures were being kept at bay but also because she appreciated the actual help Luke was now giving her. He did not actively discuss the night visitors, but this was not necessary for Morgana to appreciate his support and protection.

The Van Klausen case illustrates the vital need that people who are caught up in the terrifying phenomenon of bedroom visitations have for family support. Another type of family support springs from knowledge of older family members who come from Old World cultures that recognize various types of harassing entities as real. In the case of "Janet" from Florida, for example, the young witness received support and advice from her Slovenian grandmother in dealing with a terrifying creature who repeatedly harassed her at night. Her grandmother had been harassed by a similar bedroom visitor in her younger days and even had a specific nature for the creature, *medved*. She knew a specific resistance technique to fend it off and taught it to Janet (see Technique #8). Whoever or whatever these intrusive, unidentified creatures might be, they certainly constitute an actual phenomenon being experienced by humans on some as-yet-unidentified level of reality. There are thousands of such reports from rational witnesses, and these experiencers urgently need help.

Support from Family Members is one of the most accessible and natural means of help. The old adage, "two heads are better than one," applies here in a unique way. There is growing evidence collected by abduction researchers that the phenomenon is generational in nature, and parents or older generations of experiencers may know ways of combating the visitors, such as in the case of Janet. In any kind of trouble or distress, a person naturally reaches out first to family members. It is difficult to imagine the added stress and confusion experiencers feel when family members or close friends do not believe them and offer no help.

But the support of family members must be directed precisely toward solving the actual problem of the *visitations* to be effective, not merely directed toward the witnesses' emotional trauma. In the case of Billy Wolfe, whose family was involved in at least two full decades of repeated harassment, his mother and father were also frightened and helpless. It was Billy who took direct action to drive off the creatures with instinctual Righteous Anger and gunfire, but when his Righteous Anger turned into deep hatred of the entities and his remaining technique of Physical Struggle (gunfire) was not enough to prevent further visits, Billy became deeply depressed.

His family tried to help him by taking him to a psychiatrist, but this doctor had no knowledge of the subject of abducting aliens. He diagnosed Billy's problem as overactive imagination, and all he did was prescribe tranquilizers. Billy's parents supported him in fighting his problem, but their support was not directly aimed against the entities but rather toward Billy's despair. Therefore, it was not the type of family support that ameliorated or solved the problem, as contrasted to the positive actions of Luke Van Klausen.

It cannot be stressed strongly enough that abductees must have help. Little is known for certain about the basic nature of the creatures that harass them, but they constitute a very real problem for human beings who have developed no means of defense against them. In a later chapter we will address theories from historical sources and current research that might provide valid clues about their true nature. From the scientific work done thus far, however, we can hypothesize that encounters with entities take place in some type of altered reality. To the victims, their visits are real in every sense of the word.

## HOW TO DEFEND YOURSELF AGAINST ALIEN ABDUCTION

In any kind of stress or trouble, it is the family that a person tends to reach out to first. In the case of married couples, a close, trusting relationship with a spouse will help the experiencer to reach out. Supportive family links are highly successful if the experiencer is not ignored or ridiculed by other family members or close friends. The ridicule factor is still high in regard to UFO sightings, particularly close encounters, and even higher in regard to abduction scenarios and other types of bedroom visitations. Even now, fifty years after the start of the modern era of the UFO phenomenon, naive family members negate their relatives' experiences.

In other cases, members of the family believe the witness is experiencing strange and troubling occurrences. But they cannot offer any effective measures to help them prevent further episodes, because nothing in their life experience has given them the knowledge to deal with the situation. But since the abduction phenomenon is so widespread, everything possible should be done to strengthen an experiencer's resolve to ask for help from those closest to him or her.

In some instances, family members are not available for support, but close friends who essentially take the place of family members are available. Emily Cronin, whose repeated experiences with bedroom visitors are described in Technique #1, was successful in using Mental Struggle to fend off repeated visits from partially materialized bedroom visitors who fit the general description of greys. However, she combined her Mental Struggle technique with the technique of Support from Family Members to get permanent results. After Jan Whitley had moved to her own home, Emily began living with Toni Foxwell, a new roommate. Sometime after Toni moved in, Emily again began to experience bedroom visitors and used the Mental Struggle technique against them. Sometimes she uttered an involuntary sound from the sheer exertion of employing this technique. These slight sounds would wake up Toni, who slept in the same room. Toni could not see or otherwise detect the entities, but she would come over to Emily and ask if anything was wrong. Toni's close support would break Emily's paralysis, the high-pitched sound would end, and the entities would instantly vanish from sight. Even though Emily felt wide awake during these struggles, it is apparent that she was in some kind of as-yet-unidentified altered state, experiencing an altered reality, because Toni never saw the entities or heard the high-pitched sound. Toni's fully awake presence, showing concern and a strong desire to help, apparently broke Emily's altered state.

Another case of an experiencer who found a measure of support within her family is Jean Moncrief, who lives in Los Angeles. Jean's experiences began in 1995 when she was awakened one night by three entities who walked into her bedroom through the closet wall. They were blue in color and, to the witness, they seemed to be "young" spirits. They interacted with her in an off-hand, rather cheerful manner and she got the impression that they were out on a "joyride"—that is, interested in seeing what they could see.[1]

Jean Moncrief did not dare tell anyone about the visit, even her daughter, who shared her home with her. She knew that the UFO subject in general is virtually taboo among members of her racial group. She wrote to me: "Black folk would think I was crazy."[2] It is an established fact that the great majority of UFO sightings of all kinds, and particularly abduction claims, originate from the white population, at least in the United States. Of the more than 300 abduction cases I have investigated since 1965, only two experiencers have been black, Jean Moncrief and Rev. Bailey. And of the more than 1,500 UFO sighting reports I personally investigated in the Southern California area, only about a half-dozen have come from black witnesses.

Moncrief, who was fifty at the time of her first encounter, felt wide awake during the event. After one of the blue creatures had introduced his group to her as "the Blue People," the witness remembers little else.[3] The residual emotional trauma, however, was overwhelming. Starting the very next day, she became afraid to go to sleep at night and developed the habit of leaving on all the lights in her room, plus her bedroom television, when she went to bed. She describes herself as a relatively fearless person, but her residual fear of the closet through which the entities had entered was still overwhelming.

After the incident, she would not go in her bedroom, even during the day, unless the front door of her home was wide open, affording her a means of quick escape should she need it. She tried changing the room around so that her bed would not face the closet. The night after the blue entities appeared, she saw three butterflies in the room. Their color was a strange "electric blue." Jean explains she has been afraid of butterflies and grasshoppers since childhood: "It's like I'm seeing a deadly snake when I see a butterfly or grasshopper. Something happened in my childhood in a wheat field near the house I grew up in—I don't remember the details."[4]

This night, however, she inexplicably forgot her fear as she stared at the butterflies. She wondered what they were doing in her bedroom after midnight. Their light shone so brightly "the whole room was blue." She put out her hand in an attempt to catch one of them. Then she suddenly remembered her fear of butterflies, drew her hand back and pulled the bedcovers over her head. She has no further memories of that night.

The blue entities continued to visit her. She developed anger toward them because they were causing her sleepless nights. One night she told them to go away and, in her own words, "was very mean to them." She was ill and had recently discovered a lump in one of her breasts. Although a working woman, she did not have medical insurance and had not sought medical advice. The next night the blue entities came again, but most of that experience is blocked from her memory. All she can remember is "being floated back into the bedroom."

She remembers consciously that she was outside her third-floor apartment window as she floated back to her bed. "They had brought me from the sky," she describes. She states that she saw her body on the bed inside the room, and then remembers that the aliens were "turning" her as they put her back into her physical body. She describes: "I was waking up. . . . [It was] just like they were fitting me inside the me in bed." Next morning, she realized she did not have the lump in her breast anymore. She discovered that she had a perfectly circular mark on her left breast that was lighter in color than the rest of her skin. She also discovered that she had a persistent buzzing sound in her right ear. She states that it is somewhat like a radio signal, but has found that she "can live with it."

Other creatures besides the blue people began visiting Jean at night. The visits of some were quite unpleasant and traumatizing, unlike the "blues" whom she believes cured her of a troubling medical problem. She never shared the initial experiences with anyone, including her own daughter. It was not until several months after her first experience that her daughter happened to mention that she had been visited by "blue" entities, and that she had been frightened by the experience. Jean felt greatly relieved. She was no longer alone with her problem, and her daughter's independent description meant that she herself was not crazy. However, they were still unable to sleep at night unless the lights and the television were on. Investigation into this complex case is ongoing.

Jean Moncrief is one of a growing number of people experiencing abductions who are seeking help in fending off intrusive visitors. Unlike so many other experiencers who suffer trauma at the hands of uninvited creatures of the night, she is not content to merely cope as best she can. At the time of writing, Jean Moncrief is comforted by the knowledge that she is not alone. Although she regrets that her daughter is also caught up in the bedroom visitations, she at least feels that she is believed by someone close to her. She and her daughter sleep with the lights and television on, as both are afraid of complete darkness, but they have the support of each other.

Jean began to have recurring dreams of "sitting on the edge of an operating table and someone pushing something into the skin of my right leg" despite her screams of protest.[5] Eventually, she gave up trying to sleep in the bedroom and now sleeps in a chair in the living room. She does not sleep soundly at night, always feeling that she must be on her guard. She states:

> If I sleep too soundly, I will first get the dizziness in my head that is hard to shake off. I will have trouble breathing as though someone is sitting on my chest. My breathing and air supply are cut off and I have to fight for air. Once I feel the dizziness and the paralysis, if I don't get up on my feet right then and there I'm a goner. . . . So once I feel the dizziness or the drug-induced state taking me over, I get up at once and shake it off, and so that now works. If I ignore the dizziness they will subdue me. By then I try to run and can't run, scream and can't scream.[6]

Moncrief's assessment of the harassing night visitors is brief: "The things don't give a damn about humans," she states firmly. For the time being, she is using a combination of Mental and Physical Struggle, Righteous Anger, and Support of Family Members. She is presently sustained by the fact that her adult daughter understands her dilemma, being besieged by the same phenomenon.

She may also be helped by the fact that she remembered, during an in-depth interview, that her mother had been harassed by various types of unidentified bedroom visitors. Her mother told her that she had been able to fend them off and eventually rid herself of them by invoking the name of Jesus. When the technique of Appeal to Spiritual Personages (#8) was discussed with her, she expressed some interest in trying it. It is hoped that various means available in the Los Angeles MUFON investigative community—including medical study of her circular physical marking, judicious hypnotherapy, and counseling on various resistance techniques, including the one suggested by her mother—will succeed in ridding Jean and her daughter of the terror that these unidentified creatures are causing them.[7]

Timur, a young Muslim man who emigrated to Southern California from Iran, also instinctively used the resistance technique of Support from Family Members. His case will be explored in detail in Technique #8, but it is important to mention here that, in dealing with his traumatic experiences, he was strengthened and supported by information that came down by word of mouth from family members. His lack of residual anxiety surrounding his various experiences differs remarkably from the average American abductee. The existence of harassing, otherworldly creatures, called *Al-Jinn* in Arabic, is accepted in the Muslim culture and described in the Koran.[8] Timur is thoroughly supported by his culture, family members, and friends in his belief that jinns are synonymous with at least some types of abducting entities that harass victims in the Western world.

Timur's noticeable lack of negative emotions accompanying accounts of his contacts is probably due to the fact that, to him, the creatures were jinns, about which he had always heard from supportive family members and friends. They were not "unidentified bedroom visitors," they were from an order of intelligent creation described in detail in his own copy of the Koran and talked about freely in family conversations.

Support from Family Members is a powerful resistance technique if properly applied toward solving the situation of harassing entities. There is nothing like concerted group action, for humans by their very nature are social beings and were never intended by their Creator to face problems alone. The cultural backgrounds of many ethnic races contain invaluable information which has been passed down from generation to generation, and some of this information addresses the problem of unidentified, otherworldly creatures that attack while their victims are in altered states. The beings are called by many different names in different languages, but there is a strong possibility that they are all one shape-shifting breed, presently posing as occupants of UFOs.

# Resistance
# Technique
# #6

---

# Intuition

# INTUITION

- The earlier resistance techniques are employed the better the chances for success. Intuition breaks the progression of events before they begin.

- Perceiving the creatures' approach intuitively permits experiencers to prepare themselves emotionally for the creatures' arrival, adding confidence and strength to the resistance techniques they plan to use.

- The visitors seem to detect that their intended victims are ready to resist and often don't bother to come, knowing that their attempts will meet with failure. Perhaps they are intuitive as well.

- The Intuition technique is akin to how some soldiers on the battlefield sense the presence of the enemy or other dangers and save themselves from danger. Intuition also prevents accidents or other harm in civilian life.

- Many people are intuitive, but the talent is often suppressed in early childhood in the Western world. Have confidence that Intuition is a human talent and trust that it can be developed.

- If experiencers are not intuitive themselves, sometimes another person living in the home can sense the approach of visitors and can rouse the experiencer, ending the abduction scenario abruptly.

I N PRECEDING CHAPTERS, IT IS APPARENT that the earlier an experiencer detects the approach of harassing entities, the better resistance techniques work. Although many abductees report that they suddenly awaken aboard a craft with the abduction procedures already under way, many other experiencers often perceive a *progression of events* before the creatures take charge.

In general, the progression of events can be listed as follows:

1. The experiencers detect invisible presences, indicating that the entities' approach is imminent.
2. They experience a feeling of anxiety or the beginning of the loss of conscious will.
3. They experience paralysis, either physiological in nature or brought on by terror; that is, "frozen in fear."
4. The entities materialize, increasing the experiencer's terror.
5. The entities produce a feeling of calmness that soothes the witnesses' fear while bringing them under greater control.
6. The witnesses experience teleportation into a craft or other setting they do not recognize, and realize they have been captured.
7. If the experiencer's fear resurfaces, the creatures telepathically convey phrases such as "There is no need to fear" or "It will soon be over."
8. The entities continue with procedures, seemingly medical or otherwise investigatory in nature.

If the presence of the bedroom visitors is unpleasant to any degree, the earlier resistance or fend-off techniques are employed the better the chance of success. An unparalyzed witness can easily employ Physical Struggle, for example, while a fully paralyzed experiencer cannot. A witness who feels paralyzed but is still not calmed can employ Mental Struggle. Witnesses who are able to conquer their fear and stoutly believe that their rights are being violated can use Righteous Anger or Protective Rage effectively. And so on.

Some witnesses, however, are intuitive to the degree that they can detect the approach of harassing entities long before other experiencers can. These experiencers describe how they receive telepathic messages in their heads that the entities are on their way. Others feel various physiological effects before the entities arrival, effects that serve as an "early warning system." One well-known Los Angeles abductee, whose experiences several researchers have investigated and documented, invariably feels a prickling sensation up and down her limbs and the sides of her body, which increases during a period of forty-eight hours before the entities arrive.

In the case of experiencers who find the visitations irritating or traumatizing, an early warning can give them an advantage in making themselves ready to employ resistance techniques. In the cases of experiencers who use aromatherapeutic measures or other physical repellents against the creatures, they have time to properly apply flower essences or other "repelling" remedies. (These will be discussed in Technique #8.) Those experiencers who use Mental and Physical Struggle are able to prepare themselves emotionally for the creatures' arrival, making those measures more effective or, at best, not needed at all. The visitors often seem to detect that their intended victim is ready to fight and do not bother to come, knowing that their attempts to harass or abduct will meet with failure. (Perhaps the visitors are intuitive as well.)

The fact that resistance techniques work more effectively when the experiencer has intuitive advance warning seems to add strength to the hypothesis that the harassing visitors are from an interdimensional source instead of being fully physical and extraterrestrial. If we theorize that the entities are entering our space-time continuum from another dimension, our physical environment might be disturbed in some way that could be sensed by people whose intuitive talents are finely tuned.

Human intuition is an aspect of psychic functioning—which is described by various terms such as extrasensory perception (ESP), telepathy, and so on. Psychic functioning apparently spans the bridge between our physical universe and other realms of reality that appear to be nonphysical. Even if abductions eventually prove to be some type of bizarre psychological phenomenon, as suspected by some researchers, intuitive detection of its approach could still aid in the efficacy of various resistance techniques. Witnesses who are convinced they can prevent abduction would be able to do so even if the phenomenon springs unconsciously from within.

A good example of the Intuitive Method is that employed by Emily Cronin and Toni Foxwell, whose case is discussed in the chapter on Techniques #5. In addition to the resistance techniques of Mental Struggle and Support from Family Members employed by these two good friends, they added Intuition. As Emily's experiences continued with pasty-faced greys who harassed her night after night, she began to send out mental messages to Toni, appealing for help. Toni apparently received these silent appeals for help intuitively. While still asleep, she would become aware that Emily was going through another disturbing experience, even though she had not uttered any sound. Toni would then wake up and ask Emily if she needed help. This simple action broke the episodes each time, and soon Emily was free of the visitations entirely.

Unlike most family members or close friends, Toni Foxwell expresses a serious desire to encounter otherworldly creatures herself. She has delved deeply into metaphysics and is convinced that other intelligent orders of creation exist who are not normally visible in our own space-time. She was naturally curious about the creatures Emily viewed so often but which she herself never saw. She is a steadfast person who has complete confidence that she would never be induced to be taken against her will. Yet she has never had any kind of UFO sighting or detected any sort of alien presence, in an altered state or otherwise.

Possibly Toni's "non-experience" is due to the creatures' own intuitive ability. They may have no desire to tangle with intuitive individuals who are merely curious about them—individuals they would have no chance to work their will upon. In other words, Toni's extreme curiosity to know more about the creatures who traumatized Emily possibly protected her from being contacted herself. The deceitful and crafty nature of many of these creatures might impel them to avoid persons like Toni, who wishes to study them on her own terms in a nonemotional and objective manner.

Another striking example of the Intuition technique is an experiencer we shall call Robert Nolan. Nolan had prolonged wartime experience as a U.S. Marine in Vietnam. He discovered that he could intuitively sense the approach of the Viet Cong, and this sixth sense saved his life several times. After returning home from the war and retiring from the Marines, he began to experience encounters at night with large-headed creatures who intruded into his bedroom. These typical large-eyed greys abducted him into what he could only describe as "other environments" where they performed invasive procedures such as have been described by numerous other abductees.

The experiences, which began in 1987, at first took Nolan by surprise. About 1988, he decided that the visitors were disturbing his life and developed a strong desire to rid himself of them. He had not been able to form any theory to explain them and regarded them as possibly being "bad dreams." He was not in touch with any abduction researcher or support group, although he did discuss the episodes with a couple of good friends and his son, who lived in another state. He was surprised to learn that his son was experiencing the same type of phenomenon.

At the time he contacted me, he was living in an isolated area of Arizona where he enjoyed the freedom of rural living without close neighbors. The only source of electricity to his small home, for example, was a generator that broke down from time to time and demanded a great deal of effort to keep in working order. He treated these problems philosophically. "Such is the cost of 'living remotely,'" he states steadfastly. "I wouldn't trade it for town living ever."[1]

Instinctively, like Emily Cronin, he started to use Mental Struggle against the paralysis he invariably felt when the creatures were present. He did not specifically direct his focus toward the goal of moving some small part of his body, such as a finger and a toe as Emily Cronin and Melissa MacLeod did. Instead, he found that through sheer force of will he could often break the paralysis, and the creatures would abruptly vanish. At times, however, he did not use Mental Struggle soon enough and was taken from his home in what seemed to be a totally physical manner. He was never sure just where he was taken, except that there was invariably a structure like an examining table in the area, such as most abductees describe.

Events like these happened many times before he fully realized that the episodes were not just bad dreams. For two nights previous to the encounter that finally convinced him he detected vague symptoms of numbness and paralysis. Then, on the night of August 3, 1987, he awoke in a benumbed, immobilized state. He seemed to be hovering over his bed and had the distinct impression that he was either leaving or coming back from "someplace." There were three figures in his bedroom, one on the right side of his bed which was not clearly seen and one at the foot of the bed which looked as if it were wearing a hooded monk's robe. On the left side of the bed a huge pair of amber-colored eyes stared down at him.

After a great deal of effort, Nolan was able to strike out physically at the staring eyes. At this point he heard a loud popping sound and felt a kind of stunning blow to the left side of his head. He does not remember anything else and assumes he must have fallen asleep again. When he awakened the next morning he felt extremely fatigued and had a slight headache. That evening while reading the newspaper his vision started to blur, with double vision. It continued all that night; the next day his headache grew severe.

When he sought medical advice at a local Veterans Administration hospital it was found that his left ear was draining, his blood pressure was extremely high, and his blood platelet count very low. During a three-day consultation he saw a neurologist, an audiologist, and an eye specialist. It was discovered that the hearing in his left ear was almost gone completely, and it was suspected that he had suffered a stroke. Although that diagnosis was eventually ruled out, he was sent to another hospital in New York for an audio brain stem response test. There he confided in one of the doctors that his medical problems might be related to what had happened on the night of August 3. The doctor he confided in was surprisingly accepting and wanted to write it up in his report to the referring hospital. Nolan declined, but the doctor's report did mention "images."

The New York doctor diagnosed his difficulty as some kind of left-ear hearing difficulty, derivation uncertain. Nolan was then referred to other physicians who tried to find a physical source of his hearing problem. Finally he tired of incessant, nonproductive referrals. After he moved to Arizona his blood pressure and blood platelet count returned to normal, but the problem with his left ear persisted. Sometimes he felt sharp pains within the ear, which at times radiated into the center of his head and over to his right ear.

His ability to hear out of his left ear ranged from none at all to limited hearing. When he was able to hear, it seemed as if sound were coming through a thick wall. Nolan described a constant ringing or whistling sound in his ear, which sometimes "buzzed" as well. On several occasions when his night visitors came, he was awakened by a loud, crackling sound like static electricity in his left ear. On these occasions he had a sensation of the ear being touched by some type of instrument and a feeling he described as "electricity being discharged" into the ear. On such occasions he experienced sharp, lasting headaches.

During the numerous times he experienced abduction scenarios in Arizona, he often freed himself from the creatures by means of Mental and Physical Struggle. They continued sporadically, however, and he determined to permanently rid himself of them. He soon learned to sense when an encounter was about to happen, an intuitive feeling akin to the way he had detected the presence of Viet Cong—premonitions that served him repeatedly in combat.

He had experienced other types of psychic events frequently throughout his life, but had no control over them. In Robert Nolan's mind, the unidentified abducting creatures were, in a sense, enemies, for they caused him all the negative emotions he had experienced on the battlefield. Besides the mental worries, he gradually became convinced that the creatures had harmed or tampered with him in ways that left permanent physical effects. The ability to sense their presence intuitively, however, brought about a decrease in the frequency of the visits, because he was able to prepare himself to use Mental and Physical Struggle before the fact, and was not often taken by surprise. He began to use the techniques at the very first sign of "numbing," a sensation that led to paralysis. On some of the occasions when he was not so prepared, he would awake already paralyzed or find himself already "taken."

# HOW TO DEFEND YOURSELF AGAINST ALIEN ABDUCTION

Between Thanksgiving and the end of 1991 he was abducted two times. The creatures made a third attempt during this period but were not successful due to his resistance. On 6 January 1992, he was abducted again. During the process, he heard in his left ear a series of beeps. He described this as sounding like "a homing device, becoming more frequent and stronger in intensity as I arrived wherever it was they took me.

"When I got there I was placed on a table," Nolan describes. "They started to do something with my head. As I was trying to fight off the numbing state, one of them leaned over and looked at me with what seemed like some degree of concern. As it came close I could smell an almost overwhelming odor of what I took to be lilacs or maybe violets—but it seemed to be synthetic and sort of sickening."

He fought against the overpowering scent and was abruptly returned to his cabin. Wide awake, he realized that the smell was pervasive all over his nightclothes and bedding. The synthetic odor of flowers was now mixed with another odor, that seemed somewhat like burned toast. Earlier that evening a friend, Helen, had decided to stay the night and was sleeping in his bedroom while he slept on the couch in the living room. Robert went into the bedroom to try to wake his friend so she could be a witness to the flower odor. Inexplicably he could not wake her, a circumstance reported by numerous experiencers and which to date remains unexplained.

The next morning, after his friend awakened from a good night's sleep, the burned-toast odor still lingered in the cabin but the violet odor was gone. Nolan was convinced, perhaps intuitively, that the "flower smell" had been used by the creatures to mask some other odor. It seemed that he could detect some other odor besides the burned toast but did not recognize it.

The fact that he had a partial witness in his friend Helen amplified the abduction event of that particular night in his mind. He then thought back to an abduction that had occurred just after

Thanksgiving 1991. During that incident, the entities had performed some type of procedure involving the top of his head. He hesitated to call the procedure an operation, but the next morning he awoke with the top of his head pulsating, and he had a slight headache. He had the distinct impression that somehow the creatures had bored a hole in his head. He even went to the extent of looking at the top of his head in a mirror, trying to find some kind of mark, but there was none.

Although Robert Nolan still had come to no firm conclusions about the nature of the entities and the purpose of their visits, he felt they had a very advanced type of technology, so advanced they could go inside a human skull and leave no mark. By this time, he had become convinced that the entities had put an "implant" in his left ear, which he hypothesized was a homing device of some kind and the source of the "beeps" he heard.

Robert Nolan, an ex-Marine, is a stouthearted and rational human being. He is a prime example of an "experiencer" facing an unknown problem. Some type of phenomenon, which seems without doubt to be real on some level of reality, is appearing to thousands of credible people around the world. Claims of alien implants, some of which are allegedly placed deeply within the body, are frequently made by experiencers. Some of these so-called implants have been retrieved when they are close enough to the surface to be removed by people with medical expertise. To date, none of those recovered have been positively identified as extraterrestrial in nature, despite claims to the contrary.

I referred Nolan to John G. Miller, M. D., a physician and UFO researcher in the Los Angeles area who is interested in the implant aspect of abduction scenarios and in any type of physical evidence that can be checked out medically.[2] Dr. Miller's report did not show any conclusive evidence of an extraterrestrial implant.[3]

Robert Nolan had been harassed by these unidentified creatures for many years before he came to my attention. He was frightened initially by the intrusive visits when they began in 1987, but lost his fear in 1988 when he found he was able to fend off the initial approach of the creatures and even to break ongoing abduction scenarios through his own unique combination of Mental and Physical Struggle, combined with Intuition, which gave him "early warning." Once his fear diminished, he began to puzzle over why the creatures seemed so interested in him. By this time, he had read of abduction events where the witnesses were visited once or even a few times and then not bothered anymore. Nolan estimates he has been visited almost one hundred times. He does not understand what the nighttime visitors want of him and what is actually being done to him.

Most of his experiences have been recalled consciously, at least in part. At other times, he suspects that he has been abducted, with only fragmentary memories of the event. On some occasions he purposely does not use his combination of resistance techniques because his curiosity about the visitors has recently become stronger than his desire to prevent harassment. The creatures have become a matter of intense interest to him; his curiosity about them might be the main reason why the visitations continue, *because his curiosity is stronger than his determination to rid himself of them permanently.* More than one resister in my database is similarly conflicted.

At current writing, Nolan still has the ability to break off a visit when he intuitively becomes aware of the creatures' approach and when he does not wish to interact with them. He has come to a tentative conclusion, based entirely by his own independent reasoning processes, that the entities do not mean him any real harm and this seems to be the source of his ambivalence. He has not been influenced by any researcher who is convinced of any one theory or hypothesis. Indeed, he would not permit himself to be so led.

Robert Nolan has also come to the conclusion that the entities are interdimensional in nature, that is, their origin is not in our space-time continuum but rather in an alternate universe or other dimension that coexists with ours but is normally not detectable by human senses and instruments, possibly because it exists at another vibratory rate or frequency. Nolan believes in a supreme being, and describes himself as a "runaway Episcopalian." In his intense curiosity about the creatures, he sometimes wonders if the "Creative Force knows what is going on!" His years of encounters have made him keenly aware that the human mind is separate from the physical body, and he wonders at times if the reasons for the visitations is the creatures' desire to demonstrate that they are spiritual (paraphysical) beings intent on proving that there *is* a spiritual realm beyond our materialistic world. In this philosophical mode, he realizes that he has changed enormously in his thinking during the past several decades.

Intuitive detection of entity approach is not limited to Robert Nolan. Several experiencers in my current database of nearly seventy resisters detect intuitively when the entities are coming. Their intuitive aptitudes range from "telepathic messages" that UFOs can be viewed outside their homes to the more subtle process employed by Nolan and the mental communication used by Emily Cronin and Toni Foxwell.

Another example of intuitive detection is that of experiencer Lori Briggs, whose account of a 1975 abduction scenario from which she successfully escaped will be told in the next chapter on Metaphysical Methods. Since the 1980s, the creatures have made periodic attempts to reestablish contact with her. Now, however, she is intuitively alerted that the creatures are coming before they have a chance to materialize or paralyze her. Her 1975 encounter had been preceded by a piercing, high-pitched sound. Similar sounds, which often accompany paralysis, are not heard by the experiencer's spouse or roommate, which suggests that it is internal in nature. Lori has learned to detect intuitively the very beginning of the high-pitched sound, even before it is internally audible.

Her ability to detect the fact that the creatures wish to approach gives her ample opportunity to put her unique resistance technique into operation, and this prevents the creatures from coming. "Someday, perhaps," she states, "but it will be on my own time and on my own terms." Her attitude toward the unidentified beings is one of cautious curiosity, which is somewhat similar to Robert Nolan's current attitude. Lori regards them simply as an interesting order of creation, another type of intelligent creature in our vast universe.

During her one experience aboard a small craft, the creatures urged her to go with them, indicating telepathically that they wished to take her to their "mother ship." She had an intuitive feeling that if she *did* go with them it would be for breeding purposes, and, feeling that her rights were being violated, she broke off contact with them.

We can contrast Robert Nolan and Lori Briggs, two experiencers who use Intuition to strengthen their resistance techniques. Lori has stoutheartedly decided against further contact, in spite of her curiosity, and now lives peacefully. Robert Nolan's curiosity has a more ambivalent quality. His fend-off techniques work successfully whenever he employs them, but his curiosity about the nature of the creatures is ongoing and intense. Consequently, his visitors continue to come sporadically.

The success of the Intuition technique offers rather strong indications that the basic nature of bedroom visitors, specifically the creatures called greys, is interdimensional rather than fully physical. If the visitors are physical, in the sense that we ourselves are physical, the environment in which an encounter occurs would not be disturbed much by their presence because their technology would logically enable them to approach their victims quietly. However, if we theorize that the entities are entering our space-time from another dimension, our physical environment might be disturbed in some way that could be intuitively sensed by psychically sensitive witnesses. Parapsychologist Berthold E. Schwarz, M.D., suggests this in his two-volume work, *UFO Dynamics.*[4] Intuition apparently spans the bridge between our physical universe and other realms of reality.

Many people are intuitive. There is growing scientific evidence that it is a natural human talent that has been suppressed by civilization, especially in the Western world. The key seems to be to trust yourself *and* the growing evidence that Intuition is a normal human talent. There is nothing magical about it. Become an observer from the inside, trusting in your own nature. Knowledge will come from the all-knowing source—the God who created you. He is also the Creator of the harassing entities, but He desires them to stay in their own time and space and not to intrude upon the inalienable rights of human beings.

# Resistance Technique #7

---

# Meta-physical Methods

# METAPHYSICAL METHODS

- Metaphysical Methods of resistance are deliberately induced *in altered states that the witness fully recognizes as differing from everyday experience in normal space-time.*

- Envision protecting, bright white light coming from a source above you, flowing through the top of the head, spreading downward through the entire body, and extending out a few inches around you. Keep your eyes closed; the intensity of visualization is enhanced by physical relaxation.

- White light produces a protective shield over the experiencer. Persons using it "see" and "feel" the light and have confidence that it protects them from harassment.

- Metaphysical Methods are not commonly used by most humans living in Western cultures. Even so, Metaphysical Methods such as internal sound can be learned by persons who are highly motivated.

**V**ARIOUS METAPHYSICAL METHODS SEEM to be highly effective in fending off so-called alien contact. They are not unlike the Intuition technique, covered in the prior chapter, but, like Intuition, are not evident to any great degree in Western culture because these inclinations are usually suppressed in childhood. However, various Metaphysical Methods, which are effective as resistance techniques against bedroom visitors and threat of abduction, can be learned by persons who are highly motivated. Here, too, success leads to more success, probably because the witness feels the benefits of success in a totally integrated manner (mind, body, spirit).

A definition of *metaphysical* is required here, since the word might have different meanings for different readers. As used here in the context of resistance techniques, it means nonphysical, nonmaterial, disembodied, supernatural, or spiritual. The resistance techniques discussed in prior chapters—Mental Struggle, Physical Struggle, Righteous Anger, Protective Rage, and Support from Family Members—have strong physical components because the experiencers' bodies, brains, and minds are involved in "combat" in what they usually perceive as a totally physical state.[1] It is significant that the Metaphysical Methods of resistance against intrusive visitors are deliberately induced *in an altered state, which the witness fully recognizes as differing from everyday experience in normal space-time.*[2] It could be said that the experiencers realize they are fighting fire with fire!

One metaphysical technique that is commonly reported in my database is the process of "wrapping oneself with white light." Having come into common practice during the past forty years, it is frequently employed during meditation and also during hypnosis sessions by metaphysically inclined clinicians. The technique not only produces a greater degree of relaxation, which aids the hypnotic and meditative processes, but some clinicians use it specifically as a means of protecting the hypnotized client from intrusion by unwholesome forces, which they believe can gain entry into a person's psyche while in an altered state. Similarly, many persons practicing meditation either independently or in groups recognize "white light" as a protection against negative forces interfering with their quests for spiritual enlightenment.

In current spiritual literature, white light is commonly mentioned as a protective mechanism that guards against many forms of danger. These dangers can be psychological, as in emotional stress, or supernatural, as in attacks from unwholesome, nonphysical entities—variously called elementals, demons, spirit parasites—or other nonmaterial entities that people believe are attempting to assail their peace of mind. "White light" is not strictly a New Age concept. Although many books describing it are found in metaphysical bookstores, some people who follow traditional religious practices use it when deep in meditative prayer. It is a simple process that can be learned by any human being, whether they are religious, humanist, or have no particular belief in anything outside themselves. For these reasons, it is recommended highly as a resistance technique against troubling visitations.

In the mind of the person employing it, the source of the white light can be anything from a loving Creator God to a vaguer Cosmic Power. All seem equally effective, depending on the beliefs of the persons who are tapping the "source." The one requirement for "wrapping oneself in white light" is that the person using it must feel assured that it will protect him or her against unwanted visitors. As with the other resistance techniques described in this book, a firm sense of inviolable rights is required.

There are various ways of inducing the protection of white light. Some people envision bright white light as coming from a source above, flowing through the top of the head (also called the crown chakra), spreading downward through the entire body, and extending out a few inches from their body. The visualization of the light is strictly internal. It is usually necessary to keep your eyes closed, and the intensity of visualization is enhanced by physical relaxation. If you consider intrusive entities as unwholesome forces and hold the conviction that the white light technique can protect you, it can be a means of resisting contact. Several cases in my resisters' database use it successfully. Experiencers who are traditional Christians, in one denomination or another, equate "white light" with God's grace.

Other UFO researchers have discovered that white light is an effective way of protecting against bedroom visitors and abduction scenarios. Veteran UFO researcher Virgil Staff of Northern California referred me to an item in the July 1990 issue of the *Nevada Aerial Research Group* (NARG), which states in part:

> This Awareness indicates that it is possible to avoid those brain wave patterns that aliens would seek in their selection process by wrapping oneself in White Light. This Awareness suggests that in the first place, the least likely person an alien would seek would be one whose brain wave pattern indicates a socially strong and individualistic [human] entity. When you have a strong identification, knowing who in fact you really are, and have a strong connection with the spiritual essence of the highest, without much fear and without being swayed or easily influenced, you are less likely to become a candidate for abduction.[3]

The statement above concerning brain wave patterns is a NARG finding that has been independently discovered. Note, however, that they describe essentially the same personality type that succeeds in resistance as has been observed in my own database of successful resisters.

The white light technique that witnesses use as a protective shield is not "real" in a physical sense, but it *is* "real" in a nonmaterial sense. A casual onlooker cannot see the white light, but the witnesses themselves "see" and "feel" it and are convinced in their own minds that it preserves them against various dangers and harm.

Several witnesses in my database have reported that the white light technique drives off bedroom visitors, specifically the greys. Some experiencers also protect themselves beforehand, upon going to bed, with the inner confidence that the white light remains as a protective shield during sleep. Some spread the white light around the exterior of their home to assure even greater protection.

Other metaphysical techniques besides white light have been reported by successful resisters, but some are not as simple to learn. One outstanding example is that of internal sound, which was reported by Lori Briggs. She is one of the five witnesses whose abduction experiences between 1970 and 1975 are described in *The Tujunga Canyon Contacts.*

Lori Briggs is a well-educated and psychologically sound woman and a sociable and cooperative witness. She is a prime example of the reliable, productive, and honest individuals who describe abduction experiences. Her first conscious experience with bedroom visitors occurred in 1970 when she was sixteen years old. At the time she was living in Redondo Beach, California. She was sound asleep one night when she suddenly awakened fully, aware that, as she herself described it, "some force came in and just dragged me out of sleep." She felt "frozen." She could not even open her eyes at first, and sensed that there were a number of "beings" in the room. She felt herself being gently turned in bed until she was lying on her back. Disembodied voices told her that "he" was coming, that there was nothing she could do about her situation, and that she was to prepare herself to meet "someone."

Lori was bewildered. Then it seemed as though the beings allowed her to open her eyes. She saw a pair of long, thin hands, and then she stared into the eyes of an unidentifiable being standing by her bedside. She was struck by the fact that she was lying on her back with her head tilted slightly, yet she was eye-to-eye with the being. She realized that the creature had to be very short in stature, but her realization was overpowered by the look of the creature's eyes. Her sketch of this experience shows only the long-fingered hands and the staring eyes:

> That's the only thing I was conscious of. I don't even know the power those eyes had, but they were extremely intense—almost as if they were lights or something. They held me, and it seemed as if I was held in that gaze for eternity. And then everything broke—as if everything were gone. It could have lasted an hour, for all I know . . . but I don't know, because I didn't have any time sense. . . . [It] scared me, and I just hoped that nobody was going to show up. I didn't want to see anyone else. I didn't want to be visited again. I was terrified.[4]

Being very young at the time, Lori had no one with whom she could discuss the incident. She consciously remembered that audible voices in the room told her to prepare herself because "he was coming," but she could not figure out whether or not the creature into whose eyes she had gazed for what seemed like forever was the "he" she had been warned about. After the experience, she sometimes felt that she had been "out of her mind." She mentioned it to a couple of friends, but they convinced her it was some kind of a bizarre dream. Subsequently, she virtually erased it from her mind.

At the time of her second encounter in 1975, which was shared with a roommate Jo Maine (pseudonym), she had become acquainted with Emily Cronin (see Techniques #1 and #6). It was to Emily that the two young women turned for advice after their terrifying experience. Both Lori and Jo were in their early twenties and were sharing an apartment in Panorama City, California, one of the many large communities in the San Fernando Valley. Panorama City is a few miles from the Tujunga Canyon where Emily Cronin lived.

## HOW TO DEFEND YOURSELF AGAINST ALIEN ABDUCTION

Lori and Jo's apartment house seemed an unlikely place for a UFO encounter, since it faced Parthenia Boulevard, which was heavily traveled. Next to the apartment house, however, was a large empty field, the back part of which was blocked from view of the street by tall vegetation. The two friends had gone to sleep sometime around midnight when Lori was suddenly awakened by voices in the room. She glanced at the clock. It was 12:00 midnight. At first she heard the voices audibly, and then for a period of time telepathically conversed with the voices, especially with one unidentified "being" that stood close to her bed. Lori does not know how long the conversation lasted, but it seemed to be a considerable length of time. She cannot recall the initial content of the conversation but remembers vividly when the voices started to demand that she "should go with them" because they wished to "study" her.

Lori had no desire to go with them. All of a sudden, she heard a loud, high-pitched sound and realized it was coming from the creatures in the room. She also felt paralyzed. Her experience with the irritating sound, the accompanying paralysis, and the fact that unidentified bedroom visitors were insisting that she "go with them" is reminiscent of the episodes that Jan Whitley and Emily Cronin experienced in 1954. Lori and Jo did not know that Emily had had these experiences. They called her for advice because she was a trusted friend.

Lori Briggs, in 1975, was twenty-one years of age. From earliest childhood, she had an instinctive realization of what she calls her "own sound," a metaphysical technique she used to relax or meditate by concentrating on it and amplifying it at will. She used it so often and so naturally that she assumed everyone had their own internal sound.

Having matured in mind and body, and strengthened internally by frequent meditation, she was not overly frightened at the time of the 1975 visitation. By this time she had virtually forgotten the terror she'd felt during her 1970 encounter. She realized, however, that the sound produced by the entities might be able to overpower her and that she might not be able to resist the entities' insistence that she go with them. She consciously used her own sound against the creatures' irritating tone:

> The harder I concentrated on [my own sound], the louder that high-pitched sound got. I finally broke it, because I focused so much on my own sound. I broke it, it stopped, and I was released. And there I was again. I was frozen, and that's when it took everything in my power to break it. I knew I had to move, that's the only way to get out of that state. So I summoned up all my willpower, and I moved. Then it was broken.[5]

According to her conscious memories, Lori Briggs used a *combination* of resistance techniques to rid herself of the intrusive beings—first, a Metaphysical Method, her internal sound. Then, when the high-pitched sound ceased, she broke the remaining paralysis by Mental Struggle. At that point the beings vanished.

Finally able to move, she realized that all was not well with her roommate. Jo had slept soundly through the whole event, so soundly, in fact, that to Lori it seemed as though she were in a coma. Lori tried to awaken her gently, but Jo would not wake up. Lori then shook her, and finally Jo awoke. They were both puzzled. Jo ordinarily had trouble getting to sleep and was not a sound sleeper. They looked at the clock. It was one hour later, 1:00 A.M. Yet to Lori, all the events involved with the high-pitched sound and paralysis, and her struggles against them, seemed to have taken place within about five minutes. Her impression of an extended conversation was now gone.

Terrified at the unexpected event, Lori and Jo telephoned Emily Cronin at her Tujunga Canyon home. They did not know what to do or think about the inexplicable occurrence and badly needed someone they trusted to offer them sound advice. Jo had apparently slept through the whole experience, but she heard Lori describe to Emily that she had seen a whole group of little, round-headed beings in the room, most of whom had remained in the background while one of them, whom Lori assumed was the leader, stood at the bedside and conversed with her.

By the time the investigators interviewed Lori Briggs, she no longer remembered actually *seeing* the creatures in the bedroom. But Emily Cronin, who accompanied Lori to the first interview, clearly remembered the telephone call she had received in the middle of the night and the fact that Lori had described the creatures clearly. Only two or three years had passed between the 1975 incident and the beginning of the investigation, but it seemed as though Lori's memories of the event were partially erased from her mind.

The subsequent events that same night, however, were remembered by both witnesses. After Jo was fully awake, she and Lori got up and went into the kitchen. Suddenly, their ears were assailed by the high-pitched sound that Lori had heard in the bedroom. Now both young women heard it plainly. In addition to this, moments later they saw an intensely bright yellowish-white light flooding through their window. It was so bright that it lit up the entire back portion of their apartment. Its source, though unseen, seemed to be located toward the back of the field that adjoined their apartment building, in an area farthest from Parthenia Boulevard and blocked from view of the street.

When Lori and Jo called Emily Cronin to report these strange events, neither regarded it as a UFO encounter. Neither Lori nor Jo had any prior interest in the UFO subject; Lori had read only a few articles about it. They had never discussed UFOs with Emily, and it was only some time after the 1975 encounter that Emily confided the facts of her own encounters to them.

The fact that the sequence of events closely resembled other time-lapse cases that were flooding into the UFO field in the

1970s, however, prompted the investigators to regard the event as a possible encounter with UFO entities, although they did not share their suspicions with the witness. Lori, in turn, slowly began to realize independently that her 1970 incident had many elements in common with the event she'd shared with Jo.

During the initial interview, Lori Briggs seemed to withdraw into herself and sat quietly, drawing on a piece of paper. It was a small sketch of a young woman hovering over an oblong table of some kind. Beneath the table was a source of bright light that illuminated the figure. She was asked what the picture represented:

> I'm not really sure. But you were asking me about my dreams, and I started thinking about them. And I seemed to have an awareness suddenly—it happened in my brain—of being suspended, not by anything physical, but by a force, just above a very long, flat table. It was sort of pinkish, but with a transparent surface. There's a light under it. And what I think it really did was to shine through my body, and you saw the skeleton of it.

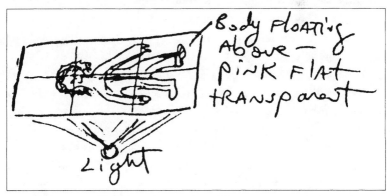

*Lori Briggs's small sketch, produced in an apparent altered state during investigators' initial interview in 1979.*

Lori's memories, surfacing entirely unaided except by her own independent concentration, were even more reminiscent of a typical missing-time episode, often involved with close UFO encounters. She stated she had no idea what the image she had drawn might mean, however, and seemed truly puzzled by it.

Plans were made for Lori to be regressed by Dr. Bill McCall. During Lori's initial hypnosis session she slipped easily into a deep trance and proved to be a superior hypnotic subject. She recalled the high-pitched, piercing sound and then the fact that a group of unidentified beings were visible in the room.

"Wow!" she exclaimed. "One of them is right next to me." This being was short, only three or four feet high, and was so unusual-looking that Lori could not be sure of its gender, but she was sure it was the leader of the others, who stood clustered by the bedroom door. It glowed with a yellow-white light and had an overly large head with deep-set, powerful eyes with no lids. The eyes were so bright that Lori felt they could hurt her if the creature wished. She was especially impressed by the physical attributes of its body, which was so thin that it seemed it would be incapable of managing its large, egg-shaped head. She also noticed that its hands had only three fingers and no thumb.

At this point in the regression session, Lori remembered being extremely impressed by the fact that the "leader" did not walk or stand on the floor next to her bed. "It's their light," she exclaimed. "Their light has lots of power." She stated that their light elevated them, and that they could direct their light through their hands to elevate other physical objects.[6] The creature demonstrated this power by elevating the lamp in the bedroom and then elevated Lori herself. At the same time she saw the creatures at the door losing their physical forms and turning into light. She was abruptly "wrapped in light" and transported *through* the wall of her bedroom into a dark, dome-shaped object that was sitting in the adja-

*Lori Briggs's sketch of one of the entities who reportedly
abducted her aboard a dome-shaped craft in 1975. Note the
feature under the chin, which Lori could not identify.
(Morgana Van Klausen also noted an unidentifiable feature
under the chin of the entity that harassed her.*

cent empty field. She received the idea telepathically that the creatures' vehicle had come from a "mother ship" orbiting somewhere in space. She found herself in a room inside their vehicle, a room that seemed much larger than it should have, since the domed craft had seemed rather small from outside. All of the features of her abduction scenario—the levitation, the passage through the bedroom wall, the inexplicable change in the size of the craft, the dematerialization of the beings—are elements common to many abduction reports.

Lori found herself lying on a table that seemed to be made of pink stone. Below where she lay was a large slot, into which the creatures from time to time inserted large slabs of similar pink stone. Each time the slot was emptied and refilled, an extremely bright source of light beneath the table shone even brighter for a short time, and the pink stone table and slab became transparent. Lori stated that she was also transparent each time the light shone brighter.

She got the impression that some type of X-ray or imaging of her body was being transferred onto the pink slabs. The entities piled the slabs against the wall as they inserted and withdrew each one. This description had many elements in common with the small sketch that Lori had drawn during her first interview, which had puzzled her because it seemed to come spontaneously from her brain, as she put it, during a period of intense concentration.

The walls of the domed craft were curved and composed of panels of a mirrorlike substance from which light emanated. Lori described under hypnotic regression how, if she looked at herself in one of these panels when the light under the table shone brightly, she could see the interior of her body. She stated that her veins and arteries seemed to be like "tubes," through which the light was flowing. She felt that she was being studied, although she was not sure what they were finding out exactly.

But I want to be able to do what they can do. They told me I can do what they can do, but I have to go with them. I don't think I want to go.

Lori's mind was filled with all sorts of impressions and what she considered "knowledge" about what was happening to her. She found it hard to describe all of this during her hypnosis session, but she shared the fact that the entities did "many things with light, that was their power." Their light reportedly enabled the entities to elevate physical objects, to transform their own bodies into light in order to pass through walls and doors, and even to transport humans through the same barriers by wrapping them in their light, as they had done with her. Similarly, she tried to explain how the entities communicated audibly among themselves, but the sounds they made were so rapid and so alien that she found it hard to describe them. Whenever they communicated with her, it was telepathic—she would simply "know" what was being said.

After an indefinite stay aboard the ship, Lori felt drained and fatigued. Wishing to be relieved of the stress, she instinctively began to make her own sound. The entities seemed startled and abruptly told her it was "time to go." Lori got up from the table and pushed a button near the door of the room. The door opened, but the creatures objected, explaining that it was better for her to go back the way she came. They then wrapped her in light again, telling her that the light was "good" and "energizing" and that they did not want her to feel fatigued from the experience. "They didn't want me to have bad feelings about it," she stated.

She was transported back through the walls of the craft, then through the walls of her bedroom. She was returned to her bed, and she glanced over and saw Jo still sleeping peacefully. Her return trip, like the initial abduction aboard the craft, was almost instantaneous. Even when Dr. McCall tried to elicit details of the return trip by slowing it down through hypnotic suggestion, it could not be slowed down. Once back in the bedroom, however, the entities continued to insist that she go with them to the mother ship. They gave no explanation why they wanted her to come with them, only that she was a person "who could understand."

Lori did not accept this explanation; it was too vague and she became suspicious of their motives. She intuitively felt that they wanted her "for breeding purposes," and this was not something in which she wanted to participate. As they continued to insist that she come with them, she instinctively started to make her own sound again. The entities countered by making a high-pitched sound, as if they were trying to force their will upon her. Lori intensified her "own sound" more and more. Eventually the creatures abruptly disappeared and their sound ceased. Lori, feeling sudden terror at what had happened to her, then tried to wake up her roommate, Jo.

The metaphysical technique of "internal sound" may strike some readers as strange, but the concept of becoming aware of one's own sound is an old yogic doctrine. Vedic literature as early as 2000 B.C. discusses the subject in detail. Some internal sounds are called *nadis*, which are defined as sounds that can be heard during meditation by the meditator's "inner ear." According to these ancient teachings, when a person becomes aware of these sounds through various meditative techniques, it signifies a certain state of spiritual development.

Besides traditional yogic doctrine, there is some scientific evidence that indicates meditators can actually hear their own sound. Lori had described her own sound as being low in pitch, unlike the high-pitched sound the entities used against her. Itzak Bentov, a biomedical inventor contends that his research reveals that 156 meditators he interviewed all described their "own sounds" as being of low frequency.

Bentov hypothesized that acoustical waves are constantly set in motion within the body and that these waves are reflected from ventricles in the brain after being generated by the heart. Since the waves are often conducted into the middle ear, they can, under the right conditions, be perceived as "sounds."[7] Bentov's book, *Stalking the Wild Pendulum,* is considered controversial by scientifically oriented researchers, but his evidence cries out for replication by others. Such research would be especially useful in the UFO field, for techniques that purported to interrupt a full-blown abduction and prevent further attempts to re-abduct the same witness surely would be valuable to experiencers who are eager to learn additional resistance methods.

Lori Briggs describes her own sound as an actual sound within her. She has been aware of it as long as she can remember. She can amplify and diminish it at will and, as mentioned, uses it in times of crisis, stress, or fear in order to bring on feelings of tranquillity and of being protected. She emphasizes that her own sound is not a mantra. "Everybody has their own sound," she states. "Nobody gave mine to me. I've always had it." She has no idea at what age she discovered it or how she learned to use it.

Those persons interested in exploring internal sound should know that scouting out details on how to discover their own sounds will involve some effort. Those who are interested in exploring this particular technique can inquire at New Age bookstores in their area. Although it may take some time to perfect, it would be well worth it, for Lori Briggs's own sound is the only resistance technique she has ever used, except in the one instance when she combined it with Mental Struggle. Since 1975, the creatures occasionally try to contact her, but she invariably uses her internal sound when she first becomes aware of their intentions. The technique invariably works to prevent further episodes. The fact that she was able to actually break off an abduction scenario *in progress* is especially interesting, in view of the fact that most of the other techniques described in this book must be used during the initial approach of the entities or in the first stages of abduction.

Another Metaphysical Method that seems to be integrally involved with abduction scenarios is termed out-of-body experience (OBE) in parapsychological literature. An OBE can be defined as an event when a person perceives their consciousness, and at times an "astral" body, separate from their physical body. Though the phenomenon is still poorly understood, parapsychologists are studying it in laboratory settings, and there is growing evidence that OBEs are actual experiences occurring in an altered state of consciousness.

OBEs occur more frequently during abduction scenarios than is commonly recognized, giving us additional evidence that "abductions" occur in an altered state. Every major researcher has a subset of cases in their files in which witnesses specify that their consciousness emerged from their physical body during an abduction, and that they saw their physical body lying in bed as the aliens floated them out a window or through a door. The actual separation of physical body and the mind-consciousness is perceived by the witness in what they assume is a fully wakeful state.[8] OBEs are reported to occur in situations other than abduction scenarios, however. Some scientists who are studying OBE deny any relationship between the two phenomena, but Kenneth Ring's recent book, *The Omega Project,* is a superior work that describes corollaries between NDEs (near-death experiences), UFOEs (UFO encounters), and OBEs.[9]

All we really know to date is that many abductees and experiencers report being abducted by alien-type beings in an out-of-body state. The OBE is becoming accepted in parapsychological literature as a "real" event, reported by reliable and honest witnesses. The process of how to achieve OBE has been studied and written about in scientific literature and books for decades.[10]

Out-of-body experience is not, of itself, a Metaphysical Method of resistance. Experiencers should be aware, however, that this one type of altered-state is involved in many abduction scenarios and should learn to recognize whether or not it is involved in their own experiences. Knowledge invariably lessens trauma and anxiety. Although practice of OBE is not specifically recommended here, it may be that some highly experienced meditators and metaphysically oriented persons could try to learn the process. If a person learns how to go out of body and *return safely* to the physical body, it is possible that that person, if caught in an abduction, might be able to "escape" the abductors and return safely home.

Other Metaphysical Methods of meditation, protection, and enlightenment can be found in books on the subjects. Besides the two techniques that have been described in detail—white light and internal sound—there are others waiting to be discovered by experiencers who have the opportunity to research for themselves. But more resistance techniques have already come to light and have been used by numerous experiencers in my database. Read on.

# Resistance Technique #8

---

# Appeal to

# Spiritual

# Personages

# APPEAL TO SPIRITUAL PERSONAGES

- Appeal to Spiritual Personages is equally effective for experiencers who are fully awake and by those who are already paralyzed and in an altered state. It requires faith in a spiritual realm where compassionate forms of life exist.

- It is perhaps the most powerful technique yet discovered, since it is readily available to a majority of experiencers, and the logic behind it is backed up by all major religions of the world.

- There is solid proof that spiritual beings interact positively with human beings, as demonstrated by the miracles performed in sacred places throughout the world.

- Since verified miracles have occurred through the intercession of various holy personages, it is logical to assume that spiritual beings such as God, Jesus, guardian angels, and saints are, in some way, "in charge" of answering fervent appeals for all kinds of help.

- Just as stouthearted experiencers feel *within* themselves that they have inviolable rights, giving them the ability to protect *themselves*, less fearless individuals who *feel* protected by spiritual sources *outside* themselves are likewise protected. It is the confidence that one is protected that brings about success.

**M**ANY UFO ABDUCTION VICTIMS BELIEVE in some religion. Appeal to Spiritual Personages connected with their religion is commonly reported both by experiencers who were fully awake and by those who were already paralyzed. This technique requires firm faith in a spiritual realm peopled by compassionate and caring forms of otherworldly life. One of the main advantages of it is that experiencers do not have to be fearless to use this technique, nor do they need a strong sense of themselves as Persons with Rights. Nor do they need metaphysical training. They only need strong faith in a spiritual realm. Christ, Mohammed, the Lord God, guardian angels, the Archangel Michael, and other spiritual personages in which the experiencer has faith have been appealed to successfully. Religious artifacts also seem effective, provided the witness has faith that they hold some form of protective power.

Appeal to Spiritual Personages is perhaps the most powerful technique yet uncovered. Its strength and efficacy seem to spring from four components:

1. The technique is readily available to a majority of people, of all religions and walks of life.
2. It is easy to apply and can be used by experiencers who are fully awake during the first stages of the entities' approach, already in an altered state, or already in the stage of paralysis.
3. Acceptance of spiritual personages as real by all of the great world religions, as well as by many of the great philosophers down through the millennia.
4. General acceptance among the world's religions, great and small, that spiritual personages such as God, Jesus, Mary, Buddha, Mohammed, various saints, angels, and spiritual guides interact with and protect individual human beings.

Tradition holds that angels, saints, and other spiritual personages actually exist and are available to human beings who appeal to them for various kinds of help. We have a kind of "proof" of their existence and the fact that they interact in a positive manner with members of the human race: the numerous sacred spots on earth where verified miracles have been performed after appeals to spiritual personages, such as in Fátima, Portugal, and similar places where miracles have been performed. It is not necessary to go into detail, for the average reader can accept the fact that "miracles" have been accomplished after appeals to certain spiritual personages, such as Christ, Mary, and saints in various religions.

Because verified miracles have occurred in all the great religions of the world through the intercession of various holy personages, it is logical to assume that these spiritual personages are in some way "in charge" of answering fervent appeals for help. One is not obliged to pray for such favors from the Almighty God (whom some term God Unknowable). There are, apparently, orders of creation between God and mankind who help human beings, and in more than one major religion, certain human beings also have achieved a stage of spiritual evolution so that they can be termed "blessed" or "saintly." Some verified miracles apparently come about as a result of appeal to these spiritual personages, so they are apparently capable of aiding human beings who call upon them for help.

Since the majority of readers believe in some form of spiritual doctrine or dogma, whether it be Christianity, Judaism, Buddhism, Islam, Shintoism, or Hinduism, among others, it should be understood that the fend-off technique of Appeal to Spiritual Personages is presented here as a pragmatic resistance method rather than as a religious teaching. Witnesses don't have to have fearless personalities. What they *do* need is strong confidence in spiritual, protecting personages. A variety of spiritual personages—so many that an entire book could be written on this subject alone—have been appealed to successfully by victims of bedroom visitors, including the so-called grey.

An example of Appeal to Spiritual Personages is documented in the case of Melissa MacLeod, a Southern California resident. As described in Technique #1, she used Mental Struggle the first few times she sensed intrusive presences in her bedroom. But in one instance in the mid-1980s, she awoke paralyzed early one morning and saw a tall, black-hooded figure standing near the side of her bed. In total terror, she instinctively prayed, "God help me!" Abruptly, the creature vanished. Melissa then experienced what might be called "a second awakening," in which she came to full wakefulness and noted that the position of a wall in her bedroom against which she had viewed the creature was now farther back than during her "vision." Whether this means that the hooded creature was seen in an environment other than her own bedroom or whether the altered state in which she viewed the figure slightly modified her perception of "reality" is not known.

Black-hooded figures are fairly common in the UFO literature, enough so that they constitute, so to speak, a subclass of UFO aliens sometimes associated with abduction scenarios. The black-hooded creature never again appeared to Melissa, but the intrusive paralysis/poking sessions with the accompanying "presences" continued unabated. Mental Struggle invariably succeeded in breaking the paralytic episodes and the sense of invisible presences abruptly vanished.

Melissa is a practicing Roman Catholic who is deeply involved in various aspects of parapsychology and psychic research. In the course of her life, she developed a particular understanding and appreciation of St. Michael the Archangel. Being rather a positive thinker and an admirer of persons who took on difficult tasks, she especially admired the Archangel for his steadfast loyalty to God. It was Michael's direct action, according to some Catholic theologians, that resulted in the majority of the heavenly hosts remaining obedient to God's will, while Lucifer and his followers disobeyed Him. While various religions differ in their teachings on angels, most of the major religions teach that they are real beings, constituting a separate order of creation that is positioned between God and mankind. All angels are radiant and brilliant beings who, according to biblical passages and descriptions in the Koran, are beautifully and wonderfully made. Yet, at the time of choice in Heaven before the creation of the world, it was Michael, an archangel, who, in response to Lucifer's objection to God's decree, cried out, "Who is like God!" This brought other angels to reflect on their choice. According to Rev. Robert Fox, in *The World and Work of the Holy Angels:*

> Lucifer supported himself on his own strength, his self-will. St. Michael's strength was in the power of God, in God's will. Scripture and our feeble attempts to understand angels can come up with imagery, but always immeasurably inaccurate and short of reality. . . . St. Michael and those myriad of angels who remained faithful, had just that, FAITH. Angels with faith? Yes, they still did not see God until their trial was over and it was over in a moment as the battle took place and was consummated in a moment.[1]

The concept of Michael as "the defender against dark spirits" continues to this day. According to many theologians, the battle of St. Michael actively fighting Lucifer and his hordes, who continue to tempt human beings to join them, is taking place on earth today.

The majority of the human race, including all the great religions, many smaller denominations, and other spiritual individuals, believe in the existence of angels according to their own understanding. St. Michael the Archangel is an excellent example of a spiritual being whose basic, magnificent nature and his God-given duty of "defender against dark spirits" is more or less universally accepted. But as explained below, "dark spirits" may mean not only fallen angels but also other intrusive spirits synonymous with greys.

The Archangel's sheer steadfastness of will fascinated experiencer Melissa MacLeod. Her appreciation of St. Michael was jolted into absolute trust in his powers when a research colleague, Stephan A. Schwartz, described to her how he had experienced what he was convinced was a vision of St. Michael in physical form. He, too, was attracted to the Archangel, and he set out to draw Michael to him.

After three months of daily meditation on this quest, Schwartz was suddenly aware of a point of light that appeared in his room. Out of this point of light, the form of St. Michael emerged. Schwartz described Michael as a "Being of Light," humanoid in shape and larger than human. "He had a demeanor of absolute implacability," he told Melissa. Michael's phenomenal personality astounded him because it was so unexpected and also so profound.

Later, mulling over the unexpected aspects of the vision in his mind, Stephan Schwartz realized that implacability, involving as it does the elements of steadfastness and inflexibility, was what one should expect of St. Michael, the spiritual being whose absolute loyalty to God had brought about an end to the battle in heaven. Melissa, too, recognized that implacability was a highly desirable quality, holding within it elements of loyalty, fidelity, and determination.

Having learned this additional information about Michael during her discussion with Schwartz, Melissa decided that she would call upon the Archangel whenever she was besieged by the invisible presences. Her appeal to God had apparently gotten rid of the black-hooded creature that had terrorized her, but St. Michael seemed more accessible. Melissa came from a generation of Catholic schoolchildren who were taught to pray "the prayer to

St. Michael" at the end of each Mass. This prayer, universally recited at the foot of the altar by priest and parishioners together before the days of Vatican II, is, unfortunately, no longer said except in private prayer:

> St. Michael, Archangel, defend us in battle. Be our protection against the wickedness and snares of the Devil. May God rebuke him, we humbly pray, and do thou, O Prince of the heavenly host, by the power of God, thrust into hell Satan and all evil spirits, who wander through the world, seeking the destruction of souls.[2]

The terms "evil spirits" and "wicked spirits" reminds many people of actual demons or devils, which are commonly equated with fallen angels. Melissa herself did not feel that the intrusive entities—the invisible presences and the black-hooded creature—were directly related to Satan. However, she interpreted the prayer to St. Michael to mean that he could be equally as effective against these unknown entities, whom she regarded as "dark spirits," as he could against the "evil spirits" in the prayer, who were commonly regarded by Catholics as fallen angels belonging to Lucifer's hordes.

Once she consciously switched from the technique of Mental Struggle and substituted appeals to St. Michael the Archangel, she found that the terrifying paralysis invariably brought on by the intrusive presences broke within a few seconds. She did not need to recite the prayer, but merely appealed to him mentally with the simple phrase "Dear St. Michael, help me!" repeated several times. Mental Struggle had always been reliable in breaking the paralysis, also, but it took much longer and involved the expenditure of intense mental energy. Appeals to St. Michael were faster, easier, and held within them an even greater confidence that the episode would break. As a result, Melissa's fear of the repeated visitations lessened considerably. Even though they still occur once in a while, she no longer dreads them as she formerly did. She knows she can break them whenever they might take place.

Melissa's confidence in Michael's protection seems to be the basic equivalent of Emily Cronin's, Patsy Wingate's, and Morgana Van Klausen's confidence in themselves as Persons with Rights, which in its essential form is equivalent to self-esteem. Melissa's personality was somewhat lacking in self-esteem in her younger days. As she grew into her forties, however, she learned how to be more assertive. Taken as a whole, the experiences were beneficial to her, rather than totally negative. She regards the fact that she can drive off the presences as totally positive.

In brief, if witnesses involved in UFO encounters feel within themselves that they have inviolable rights and an ability to protect themselves, they are protected. Likewise, if witnesses like Melissa McLeod feel they can receive protection from outside sources, they are equally protected. It is the confidence that one is protected, or that particular techniques will work, that seems to bring about success.

The above assurance, however, does not apply only to witnesses who subscribe to Christian beliefs. The technique of appealing to spiritual personages has been reported by numerous witnesses who hold religious beliefs of many kinds. The majority of people would concede that many UFO abduction victims believe in some spiritual doctrine, whether it be Christianity, Judaism, Buddhism, Islam, or numerous other philosophies, such as white magic and New Age studies. To repeat a basic concept: If witnesses involved in UFO encounters feel *within themselves* that they have inviolable rights, they are protected by that knowledge. Likewise, if witnesses feel they can be protected *by a spiritual source outside themselves,* they can be protected against intrusion by bedroom visitors by reason of that certainty.

Their certainty that Spiritual Personages can protect them equates with the self-confidence that protects experiencers who successfully use Physical Struggle, Righteous Anger, and Protective Rage. I would like to reiterate that a *combination* of resistance techniques are often necessary to fend off the intrusive creatures permanently, or, as in the cases of Morgana Van Klausen and Melissa McLeod, to build up the witness's sense of protection sufficiently that he or she no longer fears intrusion.

A striking example of a young Iranian man demonstrates that beliefs prevalent in Islam *and* the techniques that are passed down by word of mouth permit members of that faith to fight off attacks by otherworldly creatures. I investigated this case with Georgeanne Cifarelli, who is presently assistant director for MUFON in Southern California. The witness, Timur, described his experience with two type of harassing creatures. These, and others in the order of intelligent creation, called *"Al-Jinn"* in Arabic, fit neatly into the intrusive bedroom-visitor puzzle.

At the time he was experiencing the events involving intrusive entities, Timur was attending college and also working part-time at his first job. Like many Iranians, he is metaphysically oriented, easily accepting the reality of spiritual beings coexisting with the physical world. He believes that interaction between these worlds is normal and can result in good or bad experiences, according to the type of entities encountered. He accepts the idea of out-of-body experiences and described occurrences of this nature that had happened to him personally. He explains that the order of creation called "the Jinn" exist somewhere between the class the Western world calls angels and our own order of creation, mankind. During his description of jinns and his personal experiences with them, he referred to his own copy of the Koran, written in Arabic, to look up certain passages and show us the names of the various entities he was describing.

"There are two kinds of [jinns], the friendly kind and the unfriendly kind," Timur explained. "Some of them are God-worshippers, and some of them are devil-worshippers. The Jinn and the Devil are in one chapter of the Koran, but jinns are not synonymous with devils. I remember reading in the Koran that when Mohammed, the prophet, was out doing good, preaching, some jinns appeared from below the ground, heard what he was saying, and they believed him. I guess they were good ones. They wanted to hear more about it."

In describing his experience with a type of jinn that Iranians call "the Bakhtat," Timur stated, "Bakhtat is the kind that in the middle of the night you wake up, and you feel like you cannot move. You feel like there's a mountain in your chest, and you're paralyzed."[3]

A year or two before our interview with Timur, while he was still in school, he woke up in the middle of the night, feeling as though he were suffocating. He knew he was in the presence of the Bakhtat. He could not open his mouth to breathe and could not open his eyes to see.

"I thought, 'The only hope I have is God!' I opened up my mouth with my tongue and I said, 'God!' in Farsi," Timur described. "That thing got madder, angrier, and all of a sudden it lost its power and left. And then I was released and sat up in my bed. The room was dark, but the light from the window was coming in, and I saw my Koran on top of the television, as a protection."

"I got kind of a religious feeling," Timur adds. "And then I looked around and I saw these little things. All I could see was a round hole that was pitch black, with a little figure that was half hidden between the hole and the wall. He was hiding—he or she—was hiding half the wall, and looking at me with frightened eyes, as if I 'had the power.' "

"I was scared of that thing, and that thing was scared of me. That's the funny thing." Timur assumed that the creature he saw half hidden against the wall was the cause of the suffocating attack, the Bakhtat.

"All I remember after seeing that was that I had no control over my body anymore and I fainted," he continues. "And as I was going, I remembered God, and I left myself to God. I knew I could not tolerate this anymore, or maybe that thing put a spell on me to get back with me, so I said, 'Only God can protect me,' and I let go of it."

Just as Melissa MacLeod had done, Timur sent an instinctive and powerful appeal to God for protection. Interestingly, Timur emphasized that the creatures he saw in the bedroom after he fought off the Bakhtat had narrow, elongated eyes. He described them as having "two lines for eyes," and said that they resembled cat eyes. He pointed out their dissimilarity to creatures he had encountered during another experience. The creatures in his second experience resembled the description of greys.

One thing we might learn from Timur is that the variety of otherworldly entities is far greater than the simplified lists of types found in several recent books by well-known UFO abduction researchers. The resemblance of the suffocating Bakhtat is strikingly similar to the phenomenon known in Western culture as "the Old Hag syndrome." In episodes involving "the Old Hag," the experiencers wake up from a sound sleep to find they cannot breathe, as if a great weight is pressing down on their chests. It is not illogical to speculate that the two phenomena, the Muslim Bakhtat and the Old Hag syndrome, may have the same source.

Timur's description of his Bakhtat encounter still holds one question that he himself could not answer. Was the creature he saw hiding against the wall the same Bakhtat he had driven off by invoking the name of God? This is uncertain. What *is* known, however, through long interviews with Timur and other members of

the Iranian community, is that encounters with otherworldly creatures are considered commonplace in the Muslim world.

Timur knew before he said 'God!' what was happening to him,
because of information he learned in his childhood. It is not that he
was taught formally as a child what to do if that particular occurrence happened to him, but he had heard stories. He simply knew
that when this particular strange event occurred, you had to
remember to say, "God!" It was not specifically in the Koran, Timur
explained. He had learned it through word of mouth. He thought
it might also be found in some books, but he had not read them.

My research colleague, Don Worley, aware that persons who
delve deeply into all aspects of the paranormal, both good and evil,
might be more prone than ordinary persons to "visitors from the
dark side," protects himself, his office, and his home with a cruci-
fix. He feels fully protected in this way from any negative aspects
of the abduction phenomenon, which he has researched assiduously and effectively for more than two decades.

The Lord's Prayer, also known as the "Our Father," was mentioned specifically as a fend-off technique in the highly rated, scientifically oriented *Alien Discussions: Proceedings* of *the Abduction
Study Conference.* This conference was held at MIT in 1992.[4] In a
case that was probably a UFO phenomenon (but which the experiencer reported as "satanic" in nature), a woman witness was lying
on her back in bed, inexplicably paralyzed, when a small red light
came through the bedroom wall. It examined the room, went
around the edges of her bed, and then paused over the terrified
woman. She began saying the Lord's Prayer and singing hymns
mentally. The light left, and the woman seemed convinced that the
prayers had defended her against the intruder.

A similar solution was sought and found by a correspondent of
mine from Florida, whom I will call Janet. As a child, Janet began
to have numerous experiences in the middle of the night. A frightening figure—which she finds difficult to describe because of the

sheer terror it caused her—would appear near her bed at night. In the experiencer's own words, the entity was "almost like an electronic force, trying to pull me out of my body."[5]

Janet had a special relationship of love and trust with her grandmother, and she conquered her fear enough to confide in the older woman. To her relief, she learned that the grandmother had had the same problem and had learned to protect herself with prayer. Her grandmother even gave her a name for the creature—*medved*. She told Janet that the word meant "creature that comes in the night." Janet's grandmother spoke Slovenian, a Slavic language that is related to the Russian tongue.

Janet was naturally curious how her grandmother had warded off the creature that had troubled her. The older woman described how she had appealed to various spiritual personages, such as Christ and his mother, Mary. Janet chose the Sacred Heart, a Catholic concept of Jesus that she especially revered and loved. At her grandmother's suggestion, Janet kept a picture of the Sacred Heart near her bedside.

When the creature next appeared, Janet visualized the Sacred Heart protecting her against it. According to Janet, the creature stood still. Taking advantage of this, she controlled her terror enough to ask it questions, as her grandmother had advised her to do.[6]

"Who are you?" she asked.

There was no answer from the creature.

"What do you want?" Janet asked next, visualizing the protection of the Sacred Heart around her.

Again, she didn't receive an answer. Instead, the creature came closer, right up next to Janet's face, and stared directly into her eyes. At this point Janet leaped out of her bed and ran out of the room. The creature made no attempt to follow. When Janet returned to her bed, the creature had disappeared. Janet went back to bed and slept peacefully through the night. The same actions were repeated over and over again during her childhood

*A Catholic concept of Christ, "the Sacred Heart," similar to a picture used by witness Janet during her childhood to ward off repeated bedroom visitations by an intrusive entity.*

years, but Janet felt that it was the help she had from spiritual forces, specifically the Sacred Heart, that shielded her from harm. The picture of the Sacred Heart and Janet's trust in it did not stop the creature from coming, but it gave her the self-confidence she needed to resist it each time it appeared.

The fact that the name of God, whether spoken in English by Melissa MacLeod or in Farsi by Timur, can drive away a frightening entity, is powerful information indeed. In fact, appeals to other spiritual personages in whom experiencers have particularly strong beliefs can bring similar beneficial results. *It is the confidence that one is protected that seems to work.*

Abduction researchers who are convinced that abductors and bedroom visitors are technologically superior extraterrestrials against whom members of the human race are powerless will doubtless point to the fact that Timur fainted after his encounter and really did not know what happened to him after the Bakhtat had been frightened of his power. They dismiss Timur's report that he was confident that God protected him from further harm on that occasion.

Against objections such as this, we can offer two possible answers:

1. Timur and several other witnesses who used this technique had been taught from childhood that occurrences like these happen to people, and they had also been taught that the way to take away the creatures' terrifying nature, or to end their visits entirely, is by invoking the name of God.

2. If people like Timur and Melissa are convinced in their own minds that the technique of Appeal to Spiritual Personages protects them from further harassment, and they develop peace of mind and conviction that they can

fend off future visits effectively, the main point of this book is demonstrated.

Resistance techniques are for the comfort, peace, and protection of witnesses, and people like Timur and Melissa feel such comfort, peace, and protection. They are ready, without fear, in case future visits occur. What more can they ask for? In all of earthly life, there are no absolutely positive promises.

# Resistance
# Technique
# #9

---

# Repellents

# REPELLENTS

- Herbs, flower essences, and essential oils are proving effective as resistance techniques. Experiment with these carefully, as the strengths needed for individual experiencers have not been determined.

- Yarrow, St. John's Wort, and pennyroyal, traditionally used for defense against harassing spirits, have been reported effective against harassing entities in current research. CAUTION: Pennyroyal has been used traditionally to induce abortions.

- Salt has been used traditionally as a repellent and has been used successfully by at least one experiencer. Practitioners of wicca use salt to keep away unpleasant spirits on Halloween.

- Iron bars, crucifixes, and crosses of iron have traditionally been used to ward off incubus and succubus attacks. Metal fans and bar magnets crossed over the chest have recently been reported to help against abductors. Experiment with bar magnets to attain the polarity that works best for you.

A NINTH TECHNIQUE THAT HOLDS OUT considerable promise is Repellents, which can be defined as the use of herbs, essential oils, flower essences, and specific substances such as salt and iron. These have traditionally been used in various cultures to drive off "evil spirits" or to protect the human psyche from supernatural dangers.

We have demonstrated how many respected UFO researchers now hypothesize that the problem of so-called alien abduction takes place in altered states rather than in physical reality. If this hypothesis proves valid, we are dealing with a phenomenon that affects the nonphysical essence of the human being—that is, the spirit—while at the same time it can leave physical effects in its wake. Many flower essences and essential oils work on the spirit and the astral body as well as on physical ills.

One has only to read Kenneth Ring's book, *The Omega Project*, to learn that nonphysical but nevertheless "real" out-of-body experiences (OBE) have many elements in common with what Ring terms UFOE, or UFO encounters, as well as near-death experiences (NDE—which are a main part of Ring's research but are not applicable to this book).[1] Indeed, many experiencers and abductees, either consciously or through memories retrieved through hypnotic regression, state that their abduction experiences involved their nonphysical or astral bodies while their physical bodies remained lying in bed. Jean Moncrief, for instance, describes this happening to her in Technique #5.

As to specific herbs and essential oils that might be effective as resistance techniques, researcher/experiencer Deborah Goodale Marchand reports to me that the use of aromatherapy, which encompasses the substances mentioned, has given her hope that she can find a specific substance, or a combination of substances, that will ensure protection from entities that have harassed her for years. I first met Deborah briefly in 1990 after meeting her at the 13th Rocky Mountain Conference on UFO Investigation in

## HOW TO DEFEND YOURSELF AGAINST ALIEN ABDUCTION

Laramie, Wyoming, an annual conference hosted by veteran UFO researcher and psychologist, Dr. R. Leo Sprinkle. At that conference I spoke on the subject of "resistance techniques against alien abduction," and she was the first to suggest that herbs, flower essences, and essential oils had been helpful to her. She was engaged in active research on the subject, and I corresponded frequently with her after that.[2]

During her years of research, Deborah discovered that certain substances helped in various types of negative encounters, including attempted abductions. She was generous in sharing her data for this book and provided a list of sources where products she considers reliable can be purchased. She also said that many of the substances she found beneficial can be obtained in any large health food store. As a careful researcher, she recognizes that certain herbs that might be beneficial for *her* might not work for other experiencers, and that different strengths would be necessary for different people. She makes no firm conclusions about the efficacy of any particular substances, but continues her research because of the help certain substances have seemed to provide her personally.

Deborah sent me full descriptions of various flower essences and herbs. For instance, pennyroyal (*Hedeoma pulegioides*), when used as a flower essence, eases nausea, nervous conditions, and skin problems. Traditionally it is believed to repel thought forms, especially negative ones. "Thought forms" are defined as semimaterialized forms or shapes; that is, ethereal energies translated to higher levels beyond the electromagnetic range by the power of the mind. If greys and other harassing bedroom visitors are actually from altered realities, as hypothesized by many skilled researchers, possibly the term "ethereal energies" can give us a clue to their true nature.

Pennyroyal was used by Celtic peoples to help ward off harassing faeries. Isabella Augusta Persse, who researched Celtic faery lore with William B. Yeats and wrote under her married name, Lady Gregory, records an account of a man from the Irish village of Lochlan who inexplicably lost his health and was wasting away. A local woman who was noted for curing with herbs and for protecting persons beset by harassing faeries brought him two or three leaves of pennyroyal, and the man soon became well again.[3]

Pennyroyal is also traditionally regarded as protection against psychic attack, because it reportedly strengthens one's astral body to such a degree that negative thought forms cannot penetrate the physical body. For those readers who find the interdimensional hypothesis logical as a means of explaining the origin of so-called UFO abductors, the judicious use of pennyroyal as a means of combating them presents a distinct possibility.

CAUTION: A strong word of warning is necessary regarding the use of pennyroyal. Traditionally, it was used to abort unwanted pregnancies. No information as to the amount necessary to do this is known to me, but an experiencer who is pregnant should be extremely careful in its use and consult her Ob-Gyn if she wishes to experiment with it.

Its use as a resistance technique has been very beneficial for Deborah, who stated, "I use pennyroyal at times to 'see' if what I 'feel' is real and need to be vigilant."

Yarrow (*Achillea millefolium*) is another flower essence Deborah uses when experiencing harassment. As a medicinal herb, yarrow is utilized for digestive, kidney, lung, and vaginal illnesses, but as a flower essence it is traditionally considered to offer protection from negative influences such as thought forms or extreme emotionalism. Several of the resistance techniques already described in this book require positive affirmation of *one's own ability* to succeed, along with a total lack of hatred, depression, and other negative emotions. Therefore, yarrow, which is considered effective against "extreme emotionalism," would seem worth exploring in flower-essence form.

Since pennyroyal is also considered effective against negative thought forms, the question naturally arises: Which is best, pennyroyal or yarrow, against negative thought forms? Pennyroyal deals more with actual thought forms, and yarrow is more effective in blocking "negative energy waves." Therefore, pennyroyal, for the purposes of resistance, would possibly be superior in its effect against entities that are in the process of materializing or have already materialized.

Deborah Marchand uses yarrow when she senses that "large ships are around." By this she means the carrier craft which many abductees and experiencers describe as being the source of the smaller vehicles (UFOs) onto which they are allegedly transported during abductions. The case of Lori Briggs in the preceding chapter is a splendid example of a reliable experiencer who described a mother ship (carrier craft) being involved in her abduction.[4]

Marchand also notes that St. John's Wort (*Hypericum perforatum*) might be beneficial in preventing alien abductions. As a medicinal herb, it eases burns or wounds when applied externally, and helps digestive and respiratory problems. In homeopathy, it is often used for injuries to the nerves and damaging stress. Recently in medical literature St. John's Wort has been scientifically validated as being as effective against depression as some of the widely prescribed pharmaceutical drugs, such as Prozac.[5] As a flower essence, it is traditionally regarded as a tonic that helps release fears and paranoia, including subconscious fears whose source is unknown.

St. John's Wort is also traditionally regarded as helpful in aiding the individual who astrally projects and soul travels beyond the lower astral planes to experience visionary states. It was specifically recommended as offering protection from Celtic faeries who reportedly abduct humans, according to the book *Faeries:*

> St. John's Wort is even more efficacious against spells for it provides actual protection from faeries. The St. John's Wort, being a sun symbol like the daisy, was used extensively in Midsummer pagan festivals, and is both a powerful protection and a healing plant.[6]

The benefits of experimenting with St. John's Wort would seem to be obvious for those who are traumatized by abduction scenarios. Certain herbs and essential oils were recognized traditionally as having the ability to chase off "bad faeries," "elementals," and a host of troublesome folkloric creatures, which every culture in the history of the world seems to have encountered and described, either in written word or in tales passed down by word of mouth.

Rev. Robert Kirk, a Celtic scholar who studied in depth the faery-lore of the West of Ireland and the Scottish Highlands in the seventeenth century, also studied the research of Father Sinistrari, a Catholic theologian of Padua, Italy. Sinistrari theorized an order of creation between angels and mankind. Referring to Sinistrari's work, Kirk wrote that the faery culture had laws that they were obliged by their Creator to obey. Kirk was adamant that faery folk, whom he also called "the abtruse people," were doing moral wrong by abducting human babies from their cribs and taking them away to their invisible dominions.[7]

He also took them to task for abducting young mothers so that they could nurse the children—both the stolen human infants *and* faery babies. These women were sometimes returned after long periods of earthly time, often in old age; the duration of their stay in the faery world reportedly differed from earthly time. A certain

similarity with the missing-time syndrome, which is part and parcel of present-day abduction scenarios, is apparent here.

Another resistance method that fits into the technique of
Repellents is the carrying of iron objects, which in Celtic folklore
were believed to prevent unpleasant encounters with malevolent
faeries. Some of these faeries seem to be synonymous with incubi
and succubae—the male and female spirits who delighted in sexual liaisons with humans, usually after the victim had retired for
the night. These harassing otherworldly creatures described in various cultures, are believed to be devils or demons in some
Christian denominations. In the Muslim culture, incubi and succubae are listed as types of jinns.

In medieval times, victims of incubus and succubus attacks
were advised by European clerics to keep objects of iron on their
persons in order to ward off further attacks, and in my database
several resisters state that metal objects help ward off greys. A fascinating account by researcher Nicholas A. Reiter described the
use of horseshoe magnets and Tesla coils (devices that produce
electricity presumably from telluric energy sources). He invented
a device that reportedly detected and disrupted alleged "implants"
within the bodies of abductees. Each time Reiter's device was used
in the area of the implant, the abductee reported less harassment
by the entities they assumed had implanted the device.[8]

Other examples of the use of iron objects can be cited.
Morgana and Luke Van Klausen left ceiling fans on at night, and
this seemed to help stop the harassing visits the entire Van
Klausen family experienced. Whether or not the fans actually
helped stop the visits or whether their use merely coincided with
Morgana's use of three other resistance techniques is not known.
Morgana felt that the whirling blades, heavy with metal decora-
tions, possibly prevented the creatures from entering her home.
She also suggested that the entities might be disturbed by the

swirling motion, or perhaps even feared being sucked up. Whatever the explanation, it is a technique worth trying. More than one family in my fend-off database has reported that they use metal floor fans at night to keep entities away. Of course, there is another logical suggestion—that the whirling metal fans might set up some type of electromagnetic interference that thwarts these intruders.

Another method of using metal objects—in this particular case, magnets—was told by a top abduction researcher to a scientist of my acquaintance at a UFO conference. One of the thousands of letters this high-profile researcher had received mentioned that a particular abductee held crossed bar magnets against his chest, and that this warded off the greys' approach. In general, more than one culture, including the Celtic and medieval European, advise that persons who are trying to ward off otherworldly entities should keep bars of iron—bar magnets or metal crosses—close by. The technique involving metal objects demands more research.

Another Repellent is salt. Some sources state that faeries will not touch salt because "there is danger to them in it."[9] In the UFO field, a story is currently circulating about one witness who kept her tormentors away by ringing the floor around her bed with salt. Although this technique is not as well documented as the previous ones, the information about salt is included here in the hope that some experiencers might wish to try it. It is also interesting to note that modern practitioners of wicca ring their homes with salt on Samhain (Halloween) as a traditional protection from wandering spirits.

It might be helpful to mention that the enchanting book *Faeries*, cited above, indicates that oak, ash, and thorn trees, growing together, are favorites of faeries, but that a twig from each tree bound together with red thread "is a protective charm against evil and hostile spirits." Although the book does not specify which thorn tree is involved, there are at least two that grow in Celtic countries and in England, namely blackthorn and whitethorn. Charms as resistance techniques, of course, should only be tried by those whose cultural or philosophical backgrounds permit them to believe they will be efficacious.

According to the book *Faeries*, another plant widely used in Celtic folklore to ward off bad spirits was the rowan tree. The wood was used to make butter churns, to prevent mischievous faeries from stealing the cream off the milk. The rowan tree was used far back in antiquity, to the time of the Druids, when that pagan cult was the main religion of Ireland. It was said that fires made of rowan wood could be used to conjure up spirits, which could be forced to answer important questions. Compare this with an Iranian clairvoyant who I interviewed in Southern California. She reportedly can cause jinns to materialize in a mirror and answer questions about lost objects.

On the other hand, certain herbs were traditionally thought to be *favored* by faeries. Wild thyme, for instance, was considered dangerous to humans who wished to avoid contact with other-worldly creatures, and so should never be brought inside the home.[10] Another bit of information I picked up by roaming through old volumes of faery-lore, written as historical accounts by such serious authors as William B. Yeats, Lady Gregory, and W. Y. Evans Wentz, was that persons in Celtic countries used certain heat sources to fend off harassment by bad faeries. For example, some Irish farmers put hot, glowing coals under their churns when making butter, because this reportedly prevented faeries from stealing the cream from the milk, much as a churn made from rowan wood prevented this.

The use of Repellents as a resistance technique is based on a variety of sources, including historical and folkloric. Since much folklore is based on truth, although probably tinged with embellishment, it should not be disregarded as useless. Many folkloric Repellents are identical to historical Repellents used in medieval times, and are also identical to Repellents that are proving successful when used by present-day experiencers. In the fight against unidentified intruders, no method should be discarded out of hand, even if the precise manner in which it works is unclear. Here again is an application of the unwritten law, "If it ain't broke, don't fix it!"

# What Abducting Entities in Other Cultures Tell Us About Greys

**E**VERY CULTURE IN THE WORLD SEEMS to have encountered and described, either in written word or in folktales, human interaction with deceptive and harassing creatures, variously described as elementals, faeries, *medved,* and the like. These creatures are invariably described as living in a supernatural realm that is near the earth yet not part of it. Folkloric tales carefully point out that these supernatural creatures can be both "good" and "bad" in their interactions with human beings. They reportedly have the ability to enter into our own space-time and appear temporarily physical or, alternatively, have the ability to "abduct" human beings temporarily into their own space-time(s). The American culture seems to be an exception, being a melting pot for many diverse cultural roots, with no folkloric tradition of its own. Many individual Americans, however, retain in their private lives the folkloric beliefs of their ancestors.

The realm(s) of these otherworldly creatures are described in different terms such as "planes" or "dominions," according to the age of the stories, but if carefully studied can be seen as synonymous with the modern idea of other dimensions. The term "other dimensions" originated only recently.

Mathematicians now have strong evidence that there are at least nine other dimensions besides our own space-time continuum. Science as yet has no hard physical evidence of the existence of other dimensions, but present theories are a subject of scientific study.

Several scientists and UFO researchers such as Dr. Jacques Vallee and Dr. Eddie Bullard speculate that the creatures of folklore are related to our modern UFO abducting aliens. Dr. Vallee has written several books on the UFO phenomenon, having assiduously studied the subject since the sixties.[1] He is one of the top scientific minds in the field. Vallee offered clarification on what is often referred to as "the interdimensional theory" in an interview with me.

One way to think about it would be as interdimensional, but the metaphor that I use to explain it, is if you're watching . . . TV, you'd have a very hard time explaining to a seventeenth century scientist that this image is actually going through all of us in the form of waves. It's physical, in the form of electromagnetic (EM) waves, but if you want to see it, you have to buy a television set to capture the image and to turn those waves into a picture. It's a physical signal. It's not an interdimensional or psychic thing; it's physical photons, an EM wave. . . . Now, to physicists in the seventeenth century, or even in the nineteenth century, that would make no sense whatsoever. . . . But to us it's perfectly physical and ordinary.

"UFOs could be, among other things, another level of physics. They could be a type of physical entity that knows how to manipulate space and time. . . . Most of our colleagues in ufology say, "If it's not extraterrestrial, what else could it be? Well, there are many phenomena in parapsychology, and it doesn't mean that it's necessarily "psychic stuff." These things could be more than electromagnetic phenomena. It would be more fundamental than that. I don't want to pin it down to a particular theory, because there are many things that could be proposed there. It doesn't mean that our physics is wrong. It means it is a subset of something else."[2]

Dr. Eddie Bullard is also one of the most objective researchers of the abduction phenomenon.[3] A professor of folklore at a major university, he has delved deeply into the possibility that folkloric accounts in various world cultures might be related to the present-day flood of reports from credible witnesses who describe abduction by otherworldly beings.

For the sake of our study of resistance techniques, we will confine our discussion of creatures existing in other dimensions to the Muslim jinns and the Celtic faeries, types that are considered to have both good and bad entities. It is the "baddies" with which we are concerned, as their characteristics of deception and harass-ment are strong in Celtic folklore (which seems to be at least par-tially based on truth). In the case of the jinns, they are solidly accepted by huge portions of the population in various Middle Eastern cultures, to the extent that they have rights in Muslim law and are described specifically in the Koran.

English researcher Gordon Creighton first presented the jinn hypothesis in the British journal *Flying Saucer Review,* in a 1983 article entitled "A Brief Account of the True Nature of the 'UFO Entities.' "[4] His hypothesis may well prove to be a truly seminal piece of work.

He pointed out in his "Brief Account" that Islam believes in the existence of three separate and distinct species of intelligent beings, instead of the two most commonly believed in by Jews and Christians—angels and mankind. Creighton, an accomplished lin-guist, has some familiarity with about thirty languages; more important, he speaks and writes about a dozen of them well. It was through his facility with Arabic that he became interested in the Muslim concept of jinns. The Jinn, according to the Koran, was the second order of intelligent creation, positioned between angels and mankind.

Creighton's close association with some Arab Muslims gave him additional information to which persons in the Western world are not ordinarily privy. The Muslims guard their concept of jinns when speaking with non-Muslims. I ran into this myself while investigating the case of Timur, and it was only through Georgeanne Cifarelli's and my acquaintance with Timur that I was allowed to obtain additional information from other members of the Iranian community in Southern California. The information coincided squarely with Creighton's own research on the subject.

Gordon Creighton, however, because of his ability to read and speak Arabic and to communicate personally with Arab Muslims, gained far more knowledge about the concept of jinns than has ever been gained by anyone else in the UFO field. So much, in fact, that when his article about jinns appeared, throwing light on the possible true nature and motives of the creatures known in the Western world as alien UFO abductors, his discoveries were met with almost total silence by the UFO field. Three researchers in the United States wrote to tell him he seemed to be on the right track, but only one gave him permission to publish this. The almost total silence was disturbing and mystifying as well, but it's my opinion that many UFO researchers are humanists and do not believe in God. Therefore, Creighton's suggestion of a third order of creation went against their humanist beliefs. Yet his careful research can no longer be ignored. His jinn hypothesis is so logical and answers so many of the questions which have swirled around the UFO abduction phenomenon that it is all important to discuss it here.

I quote freely from Creighton's seminal article because of the importance I place upon his research. It throws light upon the puzzling problem of the entities that are assumed by so many UFO researchers to be extraterrestrial in nature, and physical in our own space-time continuum. These researchers hypothesize that the greys possess advanced technology by which they seem capable of bypassing the laws of physics—dematerializing and materializing, passing through physical matter, and the like. Yet Creighton's research on jinns provides a logical hypothesis that could answer all the puzzles abducting entities pose.

I mentioned above that the Muslims regard the jinns as a third order of intelligent creation besides the angels and mankind, which are accepted by Judaism, Christianity, and various other religions. The Koran describes angels as being created out of light, and indeed it was in this form that parapsychologist Stephan A. Schwartz viewed St. Michael during his brief interlude with that heavenly Being (see Technique #8). Mankind, according to the Koran, has physical bodies of clay; that is, our bodies are composed from mineral chemical elements found on the earth, to which a spiritual essence called the spirit or the soul is joined during our earthly life.

In the Koran jinns are collectively referred to as *"Al-Jinn."* According to Creighton, most Arabic scholars consider the term *Al-Jinn* to be derived from a verb root meaning "to hide" or "to conceal." Their bodies are reportedly made of neither light nor clay, but of a substance variously translated from the Arabic as "essential fire," "essential flame," "smokeless fire," or "smokeless flame."

Shortly after the publication of Creighton's article, he received a surprising letter from one of the leading scientists in Iraq. Dr. Adil Mosa Al-Nahas had received his medical training at St. Bartholomew's Hospital in London and was head of the department of nuclear medicine at the University of Baghdad at Alwiya.

Regarding Creighton's jinn hypothesis to explain abduction scenarios, as well as certain other aspects of the UFO phenomenon, Dr. Al-Nahas wrote, "I could not find in any of my reference sources a better explanation for the UFOs than yours. They all speak of some sort of smokeless fire; a pure flame which penetrates, even the orifices of the skin, and which kills." He hypothesized that the "smokeless flame" described in Arabic sources was some sort of plasma, an energy that has not as yet been discovered by earth scientists.[5] Apparently this courageous scientist regarded UFOs, as well as the "abducting jinn occupants," to be composed of "smokeless fire."

This idea goes against my own hypothesis that there are physical UFOs (with or without intelligent life-forms aboard) surveying the earth and being caught on radar, occasionally photographed, and seen by thousands of credible witnesses that are not related in any integral way to so-called alien abductors, who seem to be interdimensional in nature and *posing* as physical UFO occupants. Yet if the Koran describes jinns' bodies as being made of "smokeless flame" or "essential fire," it would logically mean that the normal environment in which they live would also be made of this mysterious material. Possibly UFOs or craftlike objects made of "essential fire" cruise earth's atmosphere as well.

Many scientists in the UFO field theorize that physical UFOs are surrounded by some sort of plasma, which is detectable by computer enhancement in some authentic photographs as an unexplained "blurring" effect. These scientists theorize that the blurring is possibly a layer of ionized air around the craft, which might be related to its propulsion system. When seen at night, a layer of ionized air would appear as a plasma surrounding the object. So perhaps Dr. Al-Nahas is right. Too little is known at this time to draw any firm conclusions, but research continues throughout the world.

In spite of the efforts of scholars of Arabic like Dr. Al-Nahas and Gordon Creighton, the Arabic words that translate into terms like "essential fire" and "smokeless flame" remain puzzling and unexplained. Various researchers such as Chris Line, who contributes from time to time to the *Flying Saucer Review*, have speculated that "smokeless fire" and the other terms describing the material from which the bodies of jinns were created might be related to the infrared of the electromagnetic (EM) spectrum.[6] Several articles on this subject have appeared in *FSR* in the past several years, written by serious researchers.[7] True infrared is undetectable to human sight, as are, at least initially, jinns and abducting UFO entities. Therein lies the rationale for investigating the infrared to determine whether it might give clues to the true nature and source of jinns. It would also throw light (no pun intended) on the fact that some people who have been abducted, or who have had other traumatic experiences with unidentified creatures, leave lights on at night in their bedrooms or adjacent hall to keep the visitors away, as in the cases of Morgana and Luke Van Klausen and Jean Moncrief.

It stands to reason that creatures originating in the infrared, as jinns possibly do, would be overwhelmed by visible bright light and unable to function as well as they do in their usual dark environment. All through human history, in every culture, fear of the dark has been prevalent. Lighted areas were considered to be safer from various types of folkloric creatures, which fits, more or less, reports in modern-day Western culture of how alien abductors react to light.

An entirely different point concerning the EM spectrum which applies to the problem of abductors lies in the fact that the greater part of the electromagnetic spectrum is invisible to the five human senses, and most of its known parts can be detected only through sophisticated instrumentation. Whether or not the human sixth sense—variously termed intuition, ESP, telepathy, clairvoyance, clairaudience, remote viewing—is truly part of our space-time's EM spectrum is not yet known, although excellent researchers are hard at work studying the question. If it turns out that it is, then the jinn theory is strengthened, for most alien abductors communicate telepathically with their victims.

Perhaps the most revealing aspect of Creighton's article is his description of the *source* from which these creatures originate:

It seems highly likely that the source of many of them, at any rate, is not very distant from us, and some Muslim scholars who have become aware of the current Western research into the so-called "UFO Phenomenon" and have reflected awhile upon it have concluded—and I think correctly—that maybe the best way in which we can start to visualize these matters is by thinking of the Jinns as being *very close indeed to us and yet at the same time somehow very far from us. In other words, on some other dimension, or in some other Space/Time framework, "right here," or maybe in a world of anti-matter right here, or occupying as it were some other Universe that is here, behind Alice's mirror: "a mirror-*

*universe on the other side of the Space-Time Continuum," as
it has been neatly put by some investigators.*

The Qur'an [Koran], however, is not clear on this, and
admittedly it looks as though it is very possible that some of
the Jinns could be fully physical and what we call extraterrestrials, while other species of them are of an altogether
finer sort of matter, corresponding to what various UFO
investigators have tried to indicate by such terms as "ultraterrestrial" or "metaterrestrial."[8]

Creighton emphasizes that the existence of jinns is taken for
granted by the Muslim populations of the world. The questions of
their legal rights among mankind were distinctly thought out long
ago and written into Muslim law, which applies even at present.
Their legal rights include matters of marriage and of property, and
there are Muslim men today who claim to be married to jinns—
claims that are generally accepted in their culture. According to
the Koran, there are both good and bad jinns (judged from their
behavior both toward human beings and toward God the Creator).

In exploring the case of Timur and his encounters (see
Technique #8) the certainty with which the young witness spoke
when discussing the matter of the jinns had the same degree of
certitude with which a twenty-year-old American might discuss
last night's ball game. There was absolutely no equivocation, no
hesitation, only a manner of complete honesty, as if the existence
of the Bakhtat who harassed him was beyond question. And to
Timur, it was beyond question, for in his culture the experience
was as accepted and real as a traffic accident is to any American
motorist. The existence of jinns, entirely compatible with
Creighton's research, is a matter of practical reality.

With the same forthrightness that he described his traumatic
encounter with the Bakhtat, Timur also described an encounter
with another type of jinn. He had been experimenting with volun-

tary OBEs, for purposes of relaxation and exploration. He had been successful a few times, and on each occasion experienced "a kind of a buzzing and vibration between my ears as if something was vibrating in my brain."[9]

On one particular night, however, he had an involuntary OBE for which he was not prepared and actually did not want. He felt himself out of body, looking down at his physical form lying on his bed. He was facing the window and all of a sudden felt very frightened and immediately thought of jinns. Stories he had heard all his life came to mind, though he had never encountered an actual jinn during previous OBEs. As soon as he felt afraid, he immediately reentered his body.

He felt wide awake and curious about what caused his extreme fright. He decided to go out of body again, this time voluntarily. He describes vividly what happened next:

> I let myself go again. I felt myself up there, and it was like a different "plane" and on the same plane as we are right now, like projecting two different movies on the same screen. You could see both at the same time.

He felt himself being drawn toward the door leading into his bathroom, and he felt that there were two "people" standing there, but they were not human. They were small in stature, thin, and had large dark eyes. He sketched the entities for us, one from a frontal view, the other in profile.

Timur was describing otherworldly creatures that looked very much like the typical greys that reportedly abduct witnesses in the Western world. He instinctively felt that he "recognized them" from somewhere he could not remember. He felt as if they were his "lost family" and as though they were giving him "love." The love he felt toward the creatures was intense, like the love that reportedly exists between twins.

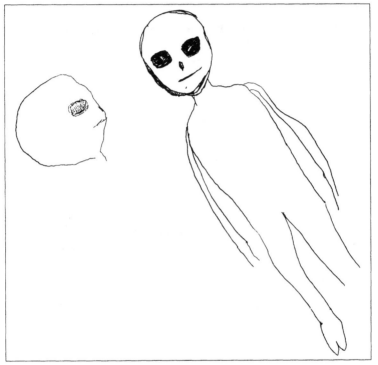

*Timur's sketch of two jinns he viewed during a traumatic out-of-body experience, possibly related to an abduction scenario.*

Timur felt absolutely no fear, even though the creatures were looking at each other and smiling as if "something had to be taken care of." He had the feeling that they were good jinns. He talked with them, saying he'd heard of creatures like them. He felt as if he were outdoors in a large field somewhere, yet also existing on another plane where he could see the features of the bathroom around him. He became concerned about what was happening with his physical body and wanted to turn around to look at it, but a sensation akin to a magnetic attraction prevented him from doing so. As he described it, a "pull" from the two entities made him continue looking their way.

The jinns were about four feet tall and grayish-brown in color. They seemed to be solid, but Timur realized he couldn't have touched them because he was out of body and didn't have physical hands. He had considerable difficulty describing their color and texture. They "were like a cloud; it's solid, but it's not solid," he stated. He was struck especially by the fact that the creatures were floating rather than walking, and seemed to be drawing him out of his bedroom to some unexplained place.

Timur was aware that he was looking at their upper bodies, because of the way they transfixed his gaze, and so his sketch does not show many details of their hands and lower legs and feet. He has an impression that the hands might have been very thin, perhaps triangular. Around the legs and feet was "very dark down there." This is a common feature found in many experiencers' sketches. Sometimes it is explained by the fact that the witness does not see the entire form because it simply isn't visible, and sometimes they simply do not notice. (It is interesting that the foot Timur *did* sketch resembled the typical "cloven hoof" depicted in portrayals of devils.)

The creatures, who Timur described without hesitation as jinns, were both demanding and loving in their attitude toward him.

> They were asking me things, instructing me. I remember they wanted my hundred percent attention, and not to look at my body on my bed. It was like telepathy. What they were saying was with love and fear at the same time. . . . Like [saying] "Sit down!" with a big smile. You feel the love, but also you feel that you're not in a position of control. Sometimes I wonder if there were more of them at my bed.

Timur described the entities as looking like UFO occupants "with the big heads" that he had seen on television. He emphasized, however, that they were not so ugly as the portrayals he had seen on TV. Their eyes were large, but round, giving them a more benevolent look than most sketches of big-eyed greys. In spite of the fact that he felt love for them, the thought continually intruded into his mind that the creatures were transfixing his attention toward them and away from his physical body on the bed.

He was worried about his body, and suspected that more of the creatures, which he could not see, might be doing something to it they didn't want him to know about. He felt ambivalence toward them, due mainly to the authoritative way they commanded his attention even though he continued to feel as if they were like his "old half."

He asked them, "Who are you? What are you doing? Why are you floating in the air? And where is the place we're going?" They replied, "Pay attention," but answered none of his questions. They kept "instructing" him, but Timur remembers no details of the instructions. Note that he had the initial feeling that they were "good" jinns, yet their actions were basically deceptive and caused him concern.

The next morning Timur woke up exhausted. He was tempted not to go to work, but got up because he knew he was obliged to. He remembered nothing about the encounter with the jinns until late afternoon. At first he thought it must be a dream, but he realized it was not a dream because it had been experienced during an OBE. The next day he discussed it with some close friends.

Following the encounter with the jinns, Timur developed a fear of going out of body. "Everytime I tried it, I didn't want to come out," he explains. This puzzled him, and he figured out that the frightening involuntary OBE *before* the jinn encounter was the reason for his fear. This was the first involuntary OBE he had ever experienced, and at the time he had felt he died. This dreadful thought made him rush back into his body to assure himself that he was still alive. Once back inside his body, with his eyes open, he felt at peace and immediately wished to "try it again."

But the resulting encounter with the jinns had somehow taken away the peacefulness previously associated with his voluntary OBEs. Timur seems not to have used any conscious resistance technique to end his encounter with the creatures he initially assumed were good jinns. Since that encounter comprised both "good" and "bad" aspects, however, it is possible that his inability to go out of body after that experience was an unconscious protective technique designed to prevent further mystifying occurrences. Timur has no memory of what happened to him after the intense, telepathic discussion with the two jinns. It is possible that a typical abduction scenario also occurred, including typical sexual tampering.

Timur described how jinns are very long-lived, that they live underground, can materialize and dematerialize into our physical space-time, have the ability to shape-shift, and can transport human beings almost instantaneously long distances. He also described that there were "two different kinds, one friendly, one nonfriendly, one with an odor associated with it and one that has no odor." Timur had no information as to which kind had the odor, but it is interesting to wonder whether or not the "burned-toast" odor mixed with the odor of "lilacs," which Robert Nolan experienced during an abduction experiences, had anything to do with a jinn (see Technique #6).

Not all of Timur's Iranian friends discuss the matter of the jinns objectively with him. "My roommate laughs at me and makes fun of me, but he was the one who was molested by these jinns when he was a kid," he states. The fact that some jinns molest human beings sexually is not specified in the Koran, but Timur explained that it was a very common thing to hear about in conversations among Iranians.

It is fascinating to compare this young Iranian-American's information with the "jinn characteristics" that Gordon Creighton lists in his *FSR* article, "A Brief Account of the True Nature of the 'UFO Entities' ":

1. In their normal state they are not visible to ordinary human sight.
2. They are, however, capable of materializing and appearing in the physical world, and can make themselves visible or invisible at will.
3. They can change shape and appear in any sort of guise, large or small.
4. They are able to appear in the guise of animals.[10]
5. They are inveterate liars and deceivers, and delight in bamboozling and misleading mankind with all manner of nonsense.
6. They are addicted to the abduction or kidnapping of humans.
7. They delight in tempting humans into sexual intercourse, and Arabic literature abounds with accounts of this kind of contact by mankind with jinn "goodies" and "baddies."
8. The jinns are wont to snatch up humans and teleport or transport them almost instantly, setting them down again . . . miles away.[11]

There are startling similarities between reports of abduction scenarios in the Western world and Gordon Creighton's excellent research on the jinns as described in the Koran. Add to this the independent description by the young Iranian-American experiencer, Timur.

Jinns are accepted without question by Muslims in the Middle East, and their existence has begun to be explored by Arabic scholars in other lands. Yet the *Al-Jinn* are not the only interdimensional order of creation that has been accepted without question by huge portions of the population in various cultures. Faery folk were widely accepted as real by the Celts.

At present, tales of faeries and the shenanigans they perpetrated for centuries upon the peoples in Ireland, especially in the more isolated middle and western counties, are treated by present-day Irish scholars as folklore—stories handed down from generation to generation that supposedly contain little reality. The western counties of Ireland have now entered into the world's economy with the rest of the Irish Republic and are no longer isolated. The legends of faery interaction still exist in the west and in other isolated places in Ireland, but, lacking scientific proof or evidence, the local inhabitants tell them simply as "stories" (except under special circumstances).

A denial by the storytellers that the events really happened is usually part and parcel of the telling. Whether this is because the current Irish storytellers' level of sophistication precludes their believing any part of the folktales themselves, or whether they prefer to hide the fact from "strangers" that they might privately believe some of the stories, is uncertain. The truth is, however, that up to about 1920, serious researchers like William B. Yeats and Lady Gregory were able to collect earnest accounts from inhabitants of Sligo, Galway, Mayo, and other western counties in Ireland because these writers were able to assure the witnesses that their accounts would be taken seriously. The two-volume work *Visions and Beliefs in the West of Ireland* is full of such accounts, told by residents in the west as actual events that happened to friends, family members, or themselves. Likewise, another Gaelic scholar, W. Y. Evans Wentz, found the faery-folklore of Ireland, Scotland, and other Celtic countries to be generally connected.[12]

Readers might ask: What is the relevance of Celtic faery-tales to the subject of resistance techniques against alien abductors? If a person carefully studies Gordon Creighton's research on the

Muslim jinn and then reads *Visions and Beliefs in the West of Ireland,* he or she will immediately be struck by the similarities of the accounts. They are so similar that Creighton writes that an early Celtic scholar, the Reverend Robert Kirk, who studied "the world of the jinn," evidently "found out *too much* and was killed by them."[13] On the other hand, W. B. Yeats, in one of his two essays in *Visions and Beliefs,* relates that Kirk died instantaneously when he stepped into the center of a "faery ring" because he had learned too much about the faery-world. Numerous other similarities found in accounts of Muslim jinns and Celtic faeries leave little doubt that the two cultures are describing similar types of beings. Creighton himself states without equivocation that the two traditions are identical.[14]

In the folklore of Ireland and of the Highland Scots, faeries are variously termed the "little people," the "wee folk," and "the Gentry." In the latter Irish designation, "Gentry" is always spelled with a capital G, just why is not precisely known. It might have been a form of flattery, designed to keep faeries from working their mischief. Or the reason might have been more subtle. The original "gentry" (small g) were aristocratic landed proprietors from England who built fine mansions in Ireland as holiday homes and "permitted" the Irish to rent small bits of their own land for exorbitant fees and taxes.

The Celtic clans arrived in Ireland about 1500 B.C., after sweeping through Europe in search of "the land they had seen in dreams." When they eventually sailed from Spain and landed in Ireland, they knew they had found the land they were seeking— their "Western hope." They displaced the race they found living on the island. Very little is known for sure about these original inhabitants except that the Irish called them "Fir Bolg," Irish Gaelic for "bag men."

To the long list of similarities between Muslim jinns and Celtic faeries could be added similarities to many other interdimensional beings described in the folklore of other cultures. For instance, the Sioux Indians living on the edge of Spirit Lake in North Dakota (mistakenly named "Devil's Lake" by the white men who first settled there in 1883) believe that the nearby woods are filled with "Canyo Tina," elflike creatures who build their homes in trees. Even at the present time, Sioux inhabitants in the area reportedly catch momentary glimpses of them scurrying by. Most other Native American tribes hold beliefs in interdimensional orders of creations, as do European and Asian ethnic groups.

For the sake of simplicity, however, jinns and Celtic faeries will be the main groups under discussion here, for the purpose of pointing out their similarities to the modern-day alien abductors. These similarities include but are not limited to the following:

1. All three types reportedly harass and traumatize human beings.
2. They reportedly materialize and dematerialize at will, pass through solid matter, and otherwise violate the known laws of physics.
3. They reportedly abduct human beings and transport them long distances in a matter of seconds.
4. They take a sexual interest in human beings.
5. They appear generally about the same size, ranging from three to four feet tall.
6. Jinns and faeries are specifically described as originating on a "hidden plane" or "other dimension" and many UFO researchers hypothesize an interdimensional origin for abducting bedroom visitors.[15]

In these six ways the three types seem identical, but other characteristics connect their behavior, lending even greater support to the theory that they are one and the same with the "third order of intelligent creation" as described in the Koran.

## HOW TO DEFEND YOURSELF AGAINST ALIEN ABDUCTION

The idea that entities abduct human beings for purposes of hybridization and genetic research is widespread in abduction literature. A possible corollary to this aspect of UFO abductor behavior is the fact that Celtic faeries, in folkloric accounts, stole human babies and took them away to faeryland where they were raised by the faery-folk. Human women were stolen to nurse both the stolen babies *and* faery babies. The thieving faeries sometimes left in the place of a stolen human infant what the Irish called a changeling; that is, a baby faery who was strange-looking, sick, and who soon died. Although these accounts of baby-stealing, nurse stealing, and changelings are not identical with present-day claims of hybrid babies, the likenesses are intriguing. Similar tales are found in the folklore of other cultures.

The six specific characteristics of faeries noted above match the characteristics of the so-called UFO alien abductors so closely that it tends to prove that alien abductors are not technologically superior extraterrestrials. Rather, it seems logical to speculate our forebears were right—that jinns, faeries, and other folkloric creatures have the capacity not only to read the minds of their victims but to shape-shift into various forms. The modern abductors often wear what appears to be space clothing and otherwise conduct themselves in a manner that leads human beings to assume they are extraterrestrial. And instead of stealing babies and women to nurse them, they now would have experiencers believe they are hybridizing our race.

Connections of Celtic faeries to modern abductors are not limited to experiencers' verbal descriptions. The set of photos that witness Rev. Harrison E. Bailey reportedly snapped of visiting entities on November 1, 1978, show a possible connection to the Celtic legends of "bag men." The pictures are admittedly controversial because of their many inherent parapsychological implications, but in spite of this many experts have studied them.

*Rev. Harrison E. Bailey's Polaroid photo depicting an
unidentified entity that materialized in his apartment on
November 1, 1978. Blurring was caused by the rapid
motion of the figure as it fled through a doorway and by
camera motion. Note "shredding effect" on right side of
figure. Copyright © Harrison E. Bailey, 1979.*

In 1993 a gifted scientist with state-of-the-art computer equipment set about enhancing Bailey's photos. One shows a small, thin-
bodied creature with a rather large head dashing through a
doorway in Bailey's apartment. Computer photo-enhancement
methods cleared up the blurred, shadowed image with rather surprising results. The picture has been essentially de-blurred, the

*Computer-enhanced version of Bailey's Polaroid photo. Note the more defined "shredding" of figure on right side, and the left arm carrying a boxlike object or "bag." Copyright © Harrison E. Bailey, 1998.*

shadows on the sides have been lightened, and the left arm is clearly seen. An object is now visible at the end of the creature's left arm, which appears to be something like a briefcase, a bag, or even a lunch box. At any rate, the entity seems to be carrying something.

A most delightful coincidence to this unexpected finding is that the ancient inhabitants of Ireland, who were displaced by the Celts, were called "bag men," or Fir Bolg in Gaelic. Some Celtic legends describe the Fir Bolg as a species of faeries and another legend relates that Ireland was built up from the seabed by the Fir

Bolg. They carried the stones, rocks, and earth that eventually created the island in bags, so it is doubly enticing to find Rev. Bailey's creature carrying what seems to be something on the order of a bag. Perhaps there is some meaning in the finding, and perhaps there is none, but one cannot help but wonder about the contents of the creature's luggage.

It is important to reiterate that some abductees or experiencers have come to terms with their bedroom visitors and have ceased to regard them as harassing or troublesome, while other experiencers have reported benevolent contacts from the beginning. Like the "good" and "bad" Celtic faeries and Muslim jinns, modern-day abductors may also have mixed motives. We are addressing witnesses who resent troubling contacts, and who wish to defend themselves against them.

A friend of mine, whom I shall call Kathleen Dreher, is Irish in ancestry and had a personal encounter with a being that fit the traditional Celtic description of "wee folk." She and her husband, Gunter, are rockhounds, and enjoy roaming mountains and deserts in search of unusual rocks, some of which contain semiprecious and precious gems in their natural state. One day several years ago, Kathleen was resting in her rocking chair in the living room when Gunter came through the kitchen to the dining room. Kathleen was astonished to see a defined, small-statured form hurrying along in front of him. She got a good look at the creature. It was humanoid in shape and about three feet tall. She stared at its clothing, for as startling as the figure itself was, its garb was even more so. It appeared to be a one-piece garment from head to toe, mulberry in color.

Kathleen's look at her husband's "companion" lasted only a few seconds, and then it vanished. As startled as she was, Kathleen was even more puzzled to realize she hadn't seen his face or hands—only the clothing. After she recovered from her astonishment, she began to wonder what the little fellow might have been, and what it was doing accompanying her husband through the house? Being a person whose mind is open to metaphysical knowledge as well as practical knowledge of the physical world, she came to an educated guess: Could the "little person" have been a gnome or faery? She had read that faeries, according to folklore, come in several types, both good and bad, and she had the impression that the one she saw was a benevolent type, perhaps a "brownie" or "nature spirit" attached to the wide, unsettled regions where she and Gunter roamed. She wondered if the little creature had, perhaps, attached itself to Gunter because it recognized that he was, in essence, a kindred spirit. Even more speculatively, she wondered if the little creature had accompanied him home with the rocks and gems over the years in order to help Gunter or, alternatively, to guard the treasures they had transplanted from their original place in nature.

Kathleen's straightforward account is not the only one I have collected from trusted friends who have confided their experiences with what would seem to be types of faeries or nature spirits. When Stephan A. Schwartz was in his twenties, he attended his first seminar on meditation and went out with a group to meditate in a state forest. Suddenly he saw a small humanoid creature resting on the large roots of a nearby tree. It seemed intensely interested in the humans gathered nearby. The little fellow was about three feet tall, and looked strikingly similar to a brownie, as they are depicted in children's faery-tale books. Schwartz was startled and puzzled; he realized he was looking at something that wasn't supposed to exist. The little creature remained for a minute or so. Then, as if aware that he himself was being observed (just as he was observing the human beings who had come into *his* woods), he vanished from sight.

Whereas some benevolent faeries seem synonymous with nature spirits, the brownie, at least in Celtic folklore, is often described as a faery that is inclined to attach itself to a human family. In many Irish folktales, a brownie decides to assist in a home where the parents are totally involved in day-to-day tasks related to raising a large family and keeping a tidy house.

They reportedly help out at night when the members of the family are asleep. They will sweep the hearth, clean the floor, tidy the kitchen, mow the hay, or perform other chores that have not been attended to due to the humans' lack of time. In exchange for a brownie's favors, the people who are helped by the obliging faery are expected to leave only a small meal, which the brownie eats at night. This is the only favor the helpful faery expects for its services.

There is an often-told Irish folktale about a household to which a brownie had attached itself. For years it helped out each night and in return was left its small meal, usually soda bread and milk. It seldom made itself seen, though it was capable of materializing fully in order to accomplish the nightly tasks. In Celtic folklore, it is explained that faeries only materialize to the extent that is necessary during each interaction with humans. (Perhaps that explains why Kathleen Dreher saw only the gnome's clothing, and not its face or hands.)

Early one morning, however, as the Irish folktale relates, the woman of the house caught a wee glimpse of "her" brownie, before it dematerialized. She noted that the little fellow's breeches and coat were ragged and badly in need of repair. She felt sorry for it, for she deeply appreciated her little helper. She knew that she could not communicate with it and offer to mend its tattered garments, so she decided instead to sew him a complete new set of clothes. When the clothes were finished, she laid them out beside his supper of bread and milk as a way of thanking him for being so helpful over the years.

Instead of accepting the clothes as a thank-you gift, the brownie was greatly offended. He regarded the gift as a hint that "his" human person thought his own clothes weren't good enough! He left the household in a huff and never returned. Later, discussing the fact that her brownie was no longer around, the woman learned from more knowledgeable neighbors that you never leave a brownie anything but a simple dinner to thank them for their services.

Not all types of brownies are desirable to have around, however. The Killmoulis, for example, a particularly homely brownie, eagerly works for millers but "delights in practical jokes and can therefore be a hindrance rather than a help."[16]

Honest accounts by reliable, sensible Americans of seeing faerylike creatures here in the United States square solidly with accounts of similar benevolent faeries in Celtic countries. Some of the accounts told to Celtic researchers emphasized that if anyone wished to attract a benevolent type of faery to one's home or property they should set out a saucer of milk and a small food offering every night. However, not all Celtic faeries are as shy as the ones reported by my friends, and setting out food is not being recommended here. Like Muslim accounts of jinns, many types of faeryfolk are unpleasantly mischievous, deceitful, and actively harassing.

W. B. Yeats, who also avidly researched accounts of faeries in Ireland during the latter part of the nineteenth century and the early twentieth century, pointed out the difficulty witnesses had in distinguishing whether the faeries they interacted with were good or bad. Sometimes it was apparent from the activities in which they involved the humans, but Yeats also uncovered a way in which observers could determine early on the true motives of the faeries they encountered. Yeats wrote of a "light" that is seen in many situations involving contact with other dimensions. In general, when this light encircles a good spirit it is usually described as white and brilliant, but about the evil spirits it is pale and "smoky."[17]

Compare Yeats's findings to what Gordon Creighton uncovered in the original Arabic that describes the *Al-Jinns'* bodies as being composed of "essential fire" or "essential flame." The descriptions of both sets of interdimensional beings are too similar to be ignored.

There are other similarities between the jinns and the Celtic faery-folk. For example, Reverend Robert Kirk, who studied Celtic folklore in the seventeenth century, specified that faeryland was "subterranean (and for the most part invisible)."[18]

Kirk, a Gaelic scholar who translated the Book of Psalms into Gaelic, also regarded faeries "as being of a middle nature between man and angels." This description is precisely the way the Muslim world describes the nature of the jinns. Furthermore, Kirk wrote that faery-folk have "intelligent, studious spirits," capable of independent thought and action, just like angels, jinns, and human beings, as described in the Koran. He also wrote that faery-folk have "light changeable bodies . . . somewhat of the nature of a condensed cloud and best seen in twilight. Their bodies are so pliable through the subtlety of the spirits that agitate them that they can make them appear or disappear at pleasure." Jinns, too, have the facilities of shape-shifting, materializing, and dematerializing in the physical world. And so do our present-day nemeses, the UFO alien abductors.

Reverend Kirk, during his intensive research, determined that the world of the faeries coexisted in some mysterious manner with our own physical world, in a way that they could use the fruits of our earth to meet their own needs, while remaining invisible to us. He described how all faeries, though essentially spirit forms with "light changeable bodies," do not all have similar bodies. Some, he writes, are "so spongeous, thin, and desiccate, that they are fed by only sucking into some fine spiritual liquors that pierce like pure air and oil," while "others feed more gross on the foisone [*sic*] or substance of corns and liquors or corn itself." In almost mystical terms, he describes how these types of more physical faeries "steal away, partly invisible, partly preying on the grain as do crows and mice."

He was careful to point out, however, that in the normal state of affairs in their order of creation, "they are empowered to catch as much prey everywhere as they please." They also occupied places on earth that were normally not accessible to man or beast.

> Their bodies of congealed air are sometimes carried aloft, other whiles [*sic*] grovel in different shapes and enter into any cranny or cleft of the earth where air enters to their ordinary dwellings, the earth being full of cavities and cells and there being no place nor creature but is supposed to have other animals greater or lesser, living in or upon it as inhabitants, and no such thing as a pure wilderness in the whole universe.

This description of the faery dominion, in a sense being "under the earth," might possibly provide a clarification of a phrase in the Bible that has always puzzled me, and doubtless has puzzled many Christians of all denominations for centuries. In Philippians 2:6–11, the Apostle Paul speaks of the name of Jesus as being so powerful that upon the mere hearing of it, "every knee must bend in the heavens, on the earth, and under the earth."

Was St. Paul referring to three orders of intelligent creation—in Heaven, on earth, and under the earth? If he was, these fit precisely with the "three orders of intelligent creation" described in the Koran—the angels in heaven, mankind on earth, and the jinn under the earth, the hidden ones. It also squares nicely with Reverend Kirk's description of three orders of intelligent creation—the angels, mankind, and the faery-folk who live "under the earth."

Greys are not a new phenomenon. They are an order of creation with the ability to shape-shift and harass human victims for their own playful or malicious motives. They have appeared in various types of garb throughout the centuries, according to the cultures in which they manifest, and appear to abductees today as extraterrestrials clad in space clothing. They are the jinns of the Muslim world, whose existence is accepted so firmly in the Middle East that they have rights in Muslim law. They are the faeries of the Celtic culture, so entrenched in Irish, Highland Scottish, and other Celtic folktales that they were feared and resisted by the inhabitants of those areas.

In her Preface to *Visions and Beliefs*, Lady Gregory unequivocably states that the Irish from whom she collected her accounts believed that the "Sidhe," as the faeries were also called, "have been, like the Angels, from before the making of the earth." She also wrote an excellent description of "faery land," which she obtained from a witness who lived in the Aran Isles, situated off the coast of Galway. This woman told her, "Those that are brought away would be glad to be back. It's a poor thing to go there after this life. Heaven is the best place, Heaven and this world we're in now."

The Celts and Muslims learned resistance techniques to help fend off the harassing attacks of "bad" faeries and jinns. So, too, some present-day experiencers and abductees have discovered techniques to resist "alien" abductors. Such success points to only one conclusion: that our own faeries and jinns are merely an old human problem, shape-shifted and wearing space garb to fool us. They can be fended off by stouthearted, determined individuals whose self-esteem is sufficient to present a confident attitude and the use of simple mental and physical techniques. It is our *own human confidence* that the intruders can be ordered to "go away" that makes these unlovely little fellows crumple .before stalwart human resistance.

# The
# Bitter
# Controversy

OTHER ABDUCTION RESEARCHERS AND experiencers are realizing that greys and other abducting entities are not technologically superior extraterrestrials from physical spacecraft. Many of these researchers and experiencers have generously contributed to this book, and special thanks is due them for their gracious help. Some experiencers were simply waiting to hear that others had used resistance successfully before speaking out. From various nations, and especially from here in the United States, stouthearted witnesses are coming forward to relate accounts of successful resistance, and more techniques—some rather surprising—keep surfacing. As a consequence, objective researchers are listening, and a few are actively trying to help experiencers who express a strong desire to get rid of their tormentors.

It is well to reiterate at this point that actual extraterrestrials from physical UFOs might be involved in a *very few* abductions, but in my opinion these cases are rare. Until we have more verified data about the nature of physical UFOs—and of bedroom-visiting, abducting greys—this remains an open question. There are many experiencers who report that the entities who interact with them are benevolent and have no reason to resist. So it is worth restating that this book describes resistance techniques that have worked successfully against *unwanted* intruders.

Abduction researchers such as Lena Miller, Donna Higbee, and others report that some of the abductees they counsel have at least partial success in fending off unwanted visitations, while other experiencers are actively seeking techniques to assert their rights. Courageous witnesses are listening to the possibilities, so they can decide whether or not they want to try to stop the contacts and which techniques might work best for them. For example, a person whose religious faith is strong and who attends church services regularly would be drawn to the technique of Appeal to Spiritual Personages; a person who has no allergies to fragrances will be more inclined to try Repellents like flower essences, and so on. A combination of techniques is valuable, too, and often essential. From preliminary study of resistance data, it seems that abducting entities, whoever or whatever they may be, may increase their efforts each time they are fended off and might even change their tactics. These factors make combinations of techniques advisable.

References to successful resistance have been tucked away in the literature, overlooked by those researchers who believe that the alien abduction phenomenon is part and parcel of the "imminent evolution" of the human race. Alternatively, other researchers firmly theorize that abduction scenarios are connected with the imminent "coming of the space beings," for more nefarious purposes, against which they believe the human race is powerless. Some of these researchers contend that the entities merely permit abductees to *believe* that their resistance techniques are successful. Until we know for certain, this possibility must be considered, of course, but those experiencers who feel they have been successful experience a peace and freedom which, for them, is equivalent to success.

But the subject of resistance remains extremely controversial in the UFO field. The inability of many researchers to believe that resistance techniques are sometimes successful is illustrated by several cases cited in *Alien Discussions,* the proceedings of the Abduction Study Conference, held at MIT in June 1992.[1] The resistance information revealed at those sessions was ignored so thoroughly that a prominent journalist who attended, C. D. B. Bryan, later wrote a best-selling book about the conference and made no mention that anyone at that well-attended, scientifically oriented gathering even mentioned the fact that some experiencers were able to resist abducting entities.[2]

Bryan's book was filled with abductees' accounts and their varying reactions to alien contact. It also contained interviews with researchers who were convinced that human beings caught up in the alien abduction phenomenon could do nothing about it except cope as best they could, as well as interviews with researchers and experiencers who accept abduction as part of a glorious extraterrestrial Great Plan. Bryan's book sold so well in hardcover that it is now available in paperback. But it tells only part of the story.

One example of resistance described in the Abduction Study Conference came from an abductee, "Lynn," who described a group of bluish-gray aliens who entered her room one night:

> They seemed angry about something. . . . This seemed to annoy me, and I asked for some help from the aliens that were helping me. The help I received helped me see that technological superiority can be no match for mind strength. At one point I grabbed one's arm just above his hand. After I saw the fear in his eyes I let go. The bluish-gray ones have not returned.[3]

Lynn reported that she "never had a negative experience" with the aliens that were abducting her regularly, even though these creatures apparently also contacted her son and husband. Her son was frightened by them, and she told him that he didn't have to go if he didn't want to. She stated that her husband complains that she "brings aliens into our room at night and he yells at me to get them out. An overwhelming feeling that he must be going crazy seems to be present."

Although Lynn must be congratulated for teaching her son a resistance technique, it seems as though the rights of her husband are being ignored. Lynn insists that her husband and children are "safe," protected by the type of aliens that are "helping" her. She claims that she has helped the aliens produce many "hybrid children" and feels "very grateful to have been involved with such an unselfish seeding of life." She feels that the aliens have not deceived her in any way. It is interesting to contrast Lynn's swift dismissal of troublesome "blue-gray" entities to the blue entities that Jean Moncrief believes healed her.

## HOW TO DEFEND YOURSELF AGAINST ALIEN ABDUCTION

The fact that Lynn recognizes that "mind-strength" is superior to extraterrestrial technology is revealing. During her one encounter with the "blue-gray aliens" she instinctively used a combination of Mental Struggle, Physical Struggle, and Righteous Anger with outstanding success. While applauding Lynn's ability to fend off the type she considered troublesome, her assessment of the "benevolent" aliens with which she interacts regularly might be questioned, in view of the historical and folkloric facts given in previous chapters. Many types of Muslim jinns and Celtic faeries are considered deceptive and mischievous, and similar creatures described in almost every culture of the world reportedly have the same deceptive nature. The intention of this book, however, is not to persuade experiencers who are satisfied with their interactions with abducting entities. It is for those witnesses who are fed up with intrusions into their lives.

Dr. Thomas E. (Eddie) Bullard recently addressed the subject of resistance, although rather briefly, in a monograph published by the Fund for UFO Research.[4] In a recent letter to me, he pointed out that many questions still surround resistance findings. He states that most experiencers probably never *try* to resist, but that those people who keep or regain some presence of mind appear best able to succeed. In his opinion the beings do not appear to be all-powerful; case records betray many vulnerabilities in their abduction procedures. Most important perhaps for the purposes of this book, Bullard states that "presence of mind" may well be the key to resistance success.[5] Presence of mind correlates nicely with confidence, self-esteem, and experiencers' conviction that their inalienable rights are being violated.

Despite the fact that successful resistance has been reported in UFO literature, it has not yet entered fully into the consciousness of most researchers, experiencers, or the public at large. The *sensational* aspect of extraterrestrial visitors interacting with helpless humans has taken over this aspect of UFO research, judging from the majority of books written on the subject, numerous television documentaries, and other coverage by the media. Could this possibly mean that stalwart humans who refuse to be harassed by otherworldly beings are not newsworthy?

It is a well-known fact that some abductees have tried *what they consider to be* fend-off techniques and have failed to drive away their harassing abductors. Likewise, most colleagues who specialize in abduction research deny that resistance techniques work. They point out examples in the UFO literature, as well as unpublished cases in their own files, where abductees have tried anger, etc., against abductors without success. For example, in the well-received book *The Allagash Abductions*, by veteran UFO researcher Raymond Fowler, an abductee reported that while he was undergoing examination by fairly typical-looking greys, he focused all his willpower and every ounce of his strength in an attempt to move his head enough to get a good look at his abductors. Even though he was young and extremely strong, he barely managed to move his head more than a inch or two. The unidentified type of paralysis that immobilized him was beyond his strength to break. As a result, this experiencer became convinced that resistance against abduction does not work.[6]

Another example is an author of another recent book on UFO abductions. When the technique of Righteous Anger was described to her by a colleague of mine, she dismissed the subject as being totally impractical. She, like many other experiencers, believes that there is absolutely no way abductees, can rid themselves of continued harassment. She admits that Righteous Anger or some other technique might temporarily chase away abducting aliens, but that invariably they come back. In her experience, even though abductees might be rid of their visits for two or three years, they nevertheless return, and upon returning their abducting methods are more assertive and become impossible to break.[7] The same view that "resistance is useless" is fairly typical of most abduction researchers.

Three aspects of the abduction problem provide at least partial answers to the above objections. First, all of the resistance techniques put forward in this book need to be carefully focused against the abductors, and this focus must contain an inherent desire on the part of the experiencers to assert their inalienable rights against intrusion. Second, there must be a total lack of hatred and negative emotion toward the entities, for any negativity directed against them lessens the effect. In other words, the focus must be totally *positive*. The "intruders" must be treated as just another order of intelligent creation that has no God-given right to harass us but is stepping out of line. Third, a combination of techniques works best.

By remaining positive, experiencers and abductees can regard the harassing visitors as other types of intelligent creatures who have been created by the same God who created humans. This implies that they have an intrinsic right to live within the normal boundaries of whatever environment their Creator gave them, but *have no right to interfere in ours*. According to the great works of philosophy and the doctrines of the major world religions, human beings were given the physical Earth to live on. This implies that, whatever or whoever abductors actually are, they also have been given their own domain.

The problem seems to be that these unidentified creatures are intruding into our earthly space-time continuum from *their own* space-time, or dimension. They do not belong here. If they did, they would be physical as we are physical. They would be detectable *at all times* by the five senses and human instrumentation.

The so-called alien abductors, however, are definitely not creatures who normally exist together with us on our physical

Earth. They reportedly have the ability to materialize and demateriaize, to pass through walls and doors in a paraphysical manner, and to intrude unbidden into our lives without our conscious knowledge, so they are not physical as we normally define the word. Human beings do not have these abilities, nor do any of the myriad of physical creatures who share our earthly realm.

When speaking of abductees and researchers who deny the effectiveness of resistance techniques, it seems almost certain that most have never even tried them with the necessary motivation and confidence. Those who have reportedly tried lacked one or more of six necessary factors:

1. Their resistance was not focused.
2. Their resistance contained an element of "hatred" toward the creatures.
3. They lacked a firm sense of their own inalienable rights.
4. They did not consider themselves capable of fighting successfully for their rights.
5. They had been instructed by researchers into thinking that the aliens are here "to evolve us" and that abducted human beings are obliged to go along with the visitors' demands.
6. They have been advised by researchers that the greys are extraterrestrial and therefore technologically and intellectually superior to humans and cannot logically be resisted.

In cases that fall into #5 and #6 above, their failure to resist must logically be attributed to the fact that most researchers do not consider the possibility that human experiencers are capable of fighting or fending off the approach of alien abductors. Certainly, the idea was not mentioned in any UFO literature, from the beginning of the present flood of abduction reports in 1973 to my initial articles on resistance techniques written between 1988 and 1992. There were mentions of resistance, of course, such as when Calvin Parker, abducted into a landed UFO by tall, robotic-type creatures, struggled against them, but soon gave in to abject terror.[8] Barney Hill, in the earliest published case of alien abduction, initially resisted and had to be dragged by the abducting entities into the landed UFO in the White Mountains of New Hampshire.[9] Some more recent books, such as Dr. David Jacobs's *A Secret Life* state resolutely that anger and rage do not work against abducting entities. And according to the cases cited in Jacobs's book, they don't.[10] But more is known now about the possible nature of abduction, and a lot of information from equally reliable witnesses who report successfully fending off abductors has surfaced over the past nine years.

The idea of the necessity of using resistance techniques without any hatred or malice toward abductors might seem strange, or even impossible, to some experiencers who have undergone years of harassment from these creatures. Like Billy Wolfe, whose case is described in Technique #2, many experiencers develop strong hatred toward the intruders. This reaction is so understandable to the majority of us that Wolfe cannot be faulted for feeling as he does. Remember that he told researcher Don Worley that he "would love to blow their heads off."

If UFO entities or bedroom visitors are truly other orders of Creation, they have a right to exist because they are God's creatures. Whether or not they give up their right to life when they invade the inviolable rights of human beings is an interesting philosophical question, which seems impossible to answer without solid evidence about their true nature. But it is possible for human beings to control their emotions and to understand the intruders' nature and motives enough to maintain a reasonably objective attitude toward them. This equable, nonhating attitude can spring from an acceptance of the intruders' basic nature and a recognition that, intrusive or not, the harassing creatures share a common origin—they have been created by the same God who created us.

Experiencers are advised to attempt to consider abducting aliens as part of God's Creation when putting into effect the resistance techniques described in this book. True, abductors are harassers and, in a sense, thieves. At the very least, they are mischievous, troublesome, and detrimental to peace of mind and body. Some may even have "evil" aspects, as abductee Billy Wolfe is convinced, a concept with which researchers Don Worley, Gordon Creighton, and others agree.

At present, however, there is only one thing that scientific methods have revealed about harassing entities: Definite *proof* of their source and motives resist all scientific attempts put forward to date. Although there are several working hypotheses put forward by skilled researchers, we have no verifiable scientific evidence that explains these entities' basic nature and their purposes in interacting with human beings. To phrase it colloquially, we seem to be stuck with them.

The best-documented cases involving reliable and honest witnesses, however, demonstrate that the abductors are a real phenomenon at some level of altered reality. They are not the result of normal dreams, fantasy, or imagination and, at least in these cases, are not explainable by any psychological aberration presently understood by science.

We can dislike their antics and we can rage against their intrusions and put into effect techniques that prevent them from violating our space, our bodies, and our minds. Once experiencers succeed in resisting them, they must forgive their trespassers as the Christian prayer "Our Father" advises. Experiencers don't have to *forget,* for they must keep up their vigilance against their possible return, but they are probably obliged to *forgive.*

## HOW TO DEFEND YOURSELF AGAINST ALIEN ABDUCTION

Noted researcher John White, author of *The Meeting of Science and Spirit,* which considers the UFO Phenomenon, puts it this way:[11]

We need to distinguish between their beingness and their behavior. As created beings in God's universe, I love them unconditionally. But love is directed at their personhood, if that term can be used for aliens. Their behavior is a different matter altogether. Although I love them unconditionally, I don't accept them unconditionally.[12]

John White gets to the heart of the matter when he addresses the behavior of the abductors, for their behavior demonstrates *the only thing* that we really know about them:

Their behavior clearly violates our own personhood. My acceptance of them is entirely conditional and must be earned. How? By demonstrating that they respect human beings as having inalienable rights. It's nothing more than the Golden Rule. If they won't respect our personhood and our property, then they're predators and deserve whatever means we can take to protect ourselves.[13]

Most of the great religions of the world share the fundamental principle that the human race is an awesome creation, and that each human individual born upon the earth is of immense value to the Creator. It may not seem that way to us, judging from the wars, poverty, homelessness, and rampant crime that we see all around us. Nevertheless, most great religions state that, in God's mind, each human person has been created for a specific purpose. Nowhere in religious texts or in the world's great philosophical works is it mentioned that unidentified beings are responsible for the evolution of the human race.

The controversy in the UFO literature regarding the efficacy of resistance techniques has been open and at times harsh. In a certain way, this state of affairs is a hopeful sign, for it might mean that ufology is approaching the status of a true science. In scientific controversies, the participants usually maintain a degree of civility when stating their objections. Sometimes, however, scientists lose their cool and exchange their conflicting outlooks in anything but a courteous manner.

Some rather sharp exchanges occurred in the *Bulletin of Anomalous Experience (BAE)*, an objective and valuable newsletter published for several years by David Gotlib, M.D., who lived and practiced in Toronto, Ontario. In June 1992, after about four years of research on resistance techniques, I wrote an article for *BAE* outlining several techniques that had surfaced during investigation of successful resistance cases. In the article, I fully recognized the controversial nature of the subject and invited the research community to contribute toward building a sufficiently large database from which statistically significant findings might be obtained. I pointed out that both positive and negative input would be appreciated.[14]

The response was immediate from several parts of the nation. Some feedback came from longtime colleagues who offered input in objective terms. Other responses, however, expressed astonishment and alarm. Several therapists involved in abduction research took umbrage at the very thought that technologically advanced extraterrestrials could be fended off by mere humans.

The first to write a Letter to the Editor was Richard J. Boylan, Ph.D., a well-known Northern California researcher. He claimed that I had made three false assumptions: that extraterrestrial contact is bad, ill-mannered or gratuitously intrusive; that very little is known for certain about the source, purpose, and motives of UFO abduction, and that this lack of information makes resistance a reasonable course of action; and that ETs have shown themselves to be deceptive in many ways.[15]

Boylan gave the example of human anthropologists who study indigenous cultures and compared this to greys who abducted human beings for study. He also wrote that the experiencers he worked with "got it." By this he meant that the experiencers he counseled recognized that the abducting entities were on an important mission that would benefit Earth, and that he himself held that view.

During my experience as a UFO abduction researcher, I have found it is wise to give credence *only to the material the witness brings to the inquiry and that any conclusion of the why and wherefore should be left up to the witness.* Most of the fully rational experiencers I work with have the ability to come to terms with their experiences on their own, with only minimum support at particularly traumatic moments. The favored hypothesis of a particular researcher should never be emphasized, for fear that the witness will consciously or unconsciously come to accept the researcher's hypothesis instead of being allowed to develop his or her own.

Researchers in the UFO field have very little verified data about the true nature of abducting beings. If an experiencer wishes to believe that the trauma caused by alien abductors will eventually serve a good purpose, he is entitled to that opinion. On the other hand, if an experiencer resents the intrusion he should have the right to fend it off in any way that works for him.

In a subsequent issue of *BAE,* I answered Dr. Boylan, pointing out that he himself was "assuming" that so-called abducting entities were extraterrestrial and physical in nature, a contention that lacks sufficient evidence to draw such a conclusion. I also pointed out that, indeed, the opposite was true—that much data pointed to the probability that the creatures were paraphysical in nature, with the ability to shape-shift, to materialize temporarily in our space-time plane, and otherwise violate the *known* laws of physics.

Dr. Dave Gotlib, editor of *BAE*, publishing all the pro-and-con input regarding the efficacy, advisability, or necessity of resistance techniques was delighted at the flow of information. The controversy continued in other venues. In 1992 I wrote about resistance techniques in the international publication, *MUFON UFO Journal*.[16] Researcher Virginia M. Tilly responded and revealed some surprising and potentially encouraging information. She had perceived a growing trend among therapists who were counseling individuals who reported they had undergone abduction scenarios:

> Just over a year ago I first became aware of this practice when several interested psychiatrists stated at a meeting that they were now giving abductees instructions that they could resist future abductions if they would only try. . . . Druffel says, "*Witnesses* are the best judges concerning the motives of entities who contact them."[17]

This has always been my position, for the witness is the one who has the experience, the one who endures the trauma. In view of the fact that little is known about the true nature of the abduction scenario, who is best qualified to be the "expert" on what it might mean—the witness who has undergone the experience or the researcher who is struggling to develop a working hypothesis? Virginia Tilly did not agree with my view on this. She continued in her "Resisting Resisting" articles:

> While it is true that ultimately each person must decide for him or herself how to respond to the experiences, there are many reasons why one's understanding about what is happening may not be clearly established. In working with such individuals it is apparent that many of them *wish* or *hope* (and often convince themselves) that the experiences are

something that fits in with their belief system. They then conduct themselves in an appropriate manner and speak with absolute conviction about what is happening to them. Upon closer inspection many often realize that the experiences have not been all that they had thought them to be.[18]

My own experience indicates that most witnesses do not "speak with absolute conviction about what is happening to them" but rather distrust alleged memories that surface, particularly under hypnotic regression. It is only after a couple of sessions that the memories begin to harden and become more acceptable to them. Ms. Tilly's response had other misconceptions, particularly about my motives in studying resistance techniques, but she put forth two important points with which I thoroughly agree. First, she revealed that psychiatrists of her acquaintance were instructing some of their patients in techniques designed to fend off unwelcome "bedroom visitors." Just what these techniques were, Tilly did not clarify, but those cases to which she referred should be collected and studied. It goes without saying that I would be glad to add them to my own database!

Second, Ms. Tilly pointed out, correctly, that many experiencers "wished" or "hoped" and often convinced themselves that the experiences are something that fit in with their belief system. She did not address this aspect of abduction scenarios in the same way I addressed it, but her comments were logical and valuable. She recognized that some abductees "have deep psychological needs to believe certain things about their abductors, whether that is for peace of mind or because of a previous belief structure."

While I do not think that psychological aberration plays a role in the majority of abduction scenarios, it is a known fact that some "potential abductees" are merely seeking attention, and consequently either imagine or wish that they had such experiences. In the UFO research field, these individuals are known colloquially as "wanabees." They are completely distinct in personality structure and motive from rational, honest witnesses who report abduction scenarios. Unlike the intellectually perceptive experiencers whose accounts are related in this book, wanabees seek attention from researchers, and the attention they are given before being recognized for what they truly are is the main reason for their abduction claims. Ms. Tilly should be thanked for bringing out this aspect of the phenomenon.

Although critical of my resistance work in general, Tilly's letter also included observations crucial to an understanding of so-called abducting entities:

> Whoever, or whatever, they are, they possess a remarkable understanding of the functioning of the human mind. The control they exert over us via mind power alone—even being able to change our perceptions of "reality"—is truly awesome. We know so little about our own minds, and use so little of our brain. But apparently our "visitors," whether through technology or some other method for which we have no comprehension, have transcended that.

The fact that some visitors are fended off initially but return with new tactics that can confound the resisters vividly illustrates Tilly's point. The apparent ability of abductors to try new tactics is the main reason why a combination of resistance techniques is usually necessary for success.

Virginia Tilly continued:

> It may also be inappropriate to assume that the process is really "for the purpose of genetic experiments, interbreeding. . . ." Again, this seems illogical. Why such a primitive method of harvesting sperm and ova? It is common knowl-

edge that such genetic material is readily available in any number of laboratories around the world. Is it possible that this too is a cover memory for something else?[19]

Although Tilly also had a different take on the above from my own, it is good that she pointed it out in such cogent terms. The reported sexual meddling by jinns and Celtic faeries—and other folkloric creatures in other cultures throughout the world—is not strictly synonymous with the sexual tamperings of the modern-day alien abductor. Tilly may have hit upon the reason. In centuries past the Celts reported that babies were taken from their cribs and faery changelings left in their places. The Irish reported that young mothers were abducted to breast-feed faery infants. And incubi and succubae took it upon themselves to engage in sexual intercourse with human beings without the humans' consent. All of these goings-on were understandable at the period of time and in the culture in which they took place.[20]

Research on the nature of abducting entities continues. It will doubtless require many more years of frank exchange between scientists and other professional researchers to come to an understanding of what these unidentified creatures really are. It does little good for one researcher to claim that he has the answer to the problem, and another researcher to claim that he has another (conflicting) answer to the problem. The vital question is: What on earth is going on? This question must be answered. Until we have verified data on the abduction problem and on the UFO problem in general, however, we are searching in the dark.

Individuals—researchers and experiencers alike—who claim they know all the answers should be careful, for certainty in the midst of uncertainty leads to chaos. The consequence of premature "certainty" will only lead us back to the 1950s and 1960s, when objective researchers and so-called contactees, who claimed to know the answers, were vying for media exposure. The objective researchers were trying to alert the public that a true phenomenon needed exploration and were searching for genuine answers to a serious scientific question, while the contactees were seeking attention for its own sake. The fatal result of that era was that the scientific community in general was so put off by the conflicting accounts that they threw up their collective hands and very few scientists did anything to help the UFO research field. Their fear of ridicule by colleagues was so great that even those who were vitally interested in the problem hesitated to join the field publicly, except for a few courageous scientists who forged ahead on their own, sometimes with disastrous results.

In like manner, the abduction phenomenon seems to be a mixed bag, with benevolent entities intermingled with deceptive ones. No one at present has all the answers. The fact that several dozen experiencers have the ability to resist harassing visitors tells us something about the nature of some bedroom visitors or abductors. If they can be fended off by simple mental and physical techniques, confidently applied by stouthearted humans, these creatures are not technologically superior extraterrestrials from physical UFOs. The phenomenon cries out for objective study and must be addressed in an unbiased manner. The past is prologue.

# NOTES

### What on Earth Is Going On?

1. Why the word is most commonly spelled "grey," as in the British spelling instead of the American spelling "gray" remains almost as much of a mystery as the greys themselves! Reports of greys originated in the United States, and it was several years before the same types of abductors were reported in the U.K. and other English-speaking countries.

2. Klass, Philip J. *UFO Abductions: A Dangerous Game.* Amherst, N.J.: Prometheus Books, 1988.

3. Fuller, John G. *The Interrupted Journey.* New York: The Dial Press, 1966. A classic book written by a well-known journalist with a scientifically oriented approach toward the UFO subject.

4. Lorenzen, Coral, and Jim Lorenzen. *Flying Saucer Occupants.* New York: Signet/New American Library, 1967, pp. 42–72.

5. I was the principal NICAP investigator on this case, having joined NICAP in 1957 just after the noted researcher-journalist Major Donald E. Keyhoe (USMC, Ret.) assumed its directorship. The case was never been made public due to the lack of scientific verification and difficulty in obtaining documentation for various aspects of the witness's account.

6. Many European "occupant" reports are published in this British journal. See *FSR: Flying Saucer Review 1955–1994: An Index,* compiled by Edward G. Stewart, 1995. This invaluable reference is available from Arcturus Book Service, 1443 S. E. Port St. Lucie Blvd., Port St. Lucie, FL 34952.

7. Details of this classic case can be found in many good UFO books. An update containing new information on the Zamora case from the files of a famous scientist and UFO researcher, Dr. James E. McDonald, will be in my book, *Scientist vs. the System: Dr. James E. McDonald's Fight for UFO Science,* publication forthcoming.

8. Druffel, Ann, and D. Scott Rogo. *The Tujunga Canyon Contacts.* Englewood Cliffs, N.J.: Prentice-Hall, 1980. Republished in paperback, and updated with two new chapters in 1988, by Signet/New American Library.

9. Druffel, Ann. "Missing Fetus's Case Solved." *MUFON UFO Journal* 283 (November 1991): pp. 8–12.

10. ———. "Support Groups: A Proposal." *MUFON UFO Journal* 234 (October 1987): pp. 11–14.

11. ———. "Abductions: Can We Battle Back?" *MUFON UFO Journal* no. 247 (November 1988): pp. 17–21, and "Resisting Alien Abductions: An Update." *MUFON UFO Journal* no. 287 (March 1992); "Resisting Alien 'Entities,'" *UFO Magazine* (1989): pp. 16–19; "Resisting Alien Abductions," *FSR: Flying Saucer Review,* Vol. 33, no. 3, September 1988, pp. 13–18.

12. McCampbell, James M. *Ufology: A Major Breakthrough in the Scientific Understanding of Unidentified Flying Objects.* Millbrae, Calif.: Celestial Arts, 1976, pp. 71–76.

### Resistance Technique #1: Mental Struggle

1. *The Tujunga Canyon Contacts,* pp. 33–35, 75–78, 106.

2. Hopkins, Budd. "A Sharp Right Turn on the National Road," in *Missing Time: A Documented Study of UFO Abductions.* New York: Richard Marek Publishers, 1981, pp. 51–88.

3. Bershad's quotes and other information about his experiences in this chapter are from my interview with him, at my Pasadena home May 26, 1997.

4. Strieber, Whitley. *Communion.* New York: Beech Tree Books/ William Morrow, 1987.

### Resistance Technique #2: Physical Struggle

1. Worley, Don. " 'Neck Breaking' Incident," Worley files, Connersville, Ind. Report prepared from taped interview. Some information on the Wingate case is from author Druffel's phone interviews and correspondence with the witness.

2. Fowler, Raymond E. *The Andreasson Affair.* Englewood Cliffs, N.J.: Prentice-Hall, 1979, pp. 23–33.

3. Worley, " 'Neck Breaking' Incident."

4. Walton, Travis. *The Walton Experience.* New York: Berkley Medallion/Berkley Publishing, 1978.

5. Ibid., p. 106.

6. Ibid.

7. Ibid., p. 107.

8. Worley, Don. "Illinois Farmer Victimized by UFO Aliens," February 10, 1990, Worley files, Connersville, Ind. Report prepared from taped interviews with witnesses.

9. Ibid., p. 4.
10. Ibid., p. 6.
11. Ibid., p. 8.
12. Letter from Don Worley to author, n.d. (1997).

### Resistance Technique #3: Righteous Anger

1. Druffel, Ann, and D. Scott Rogo. *The Tujunga Canyon Contacts.* Englewood Cliffs, N.J.: Prentice-Hall, 1980.
2. Druffel, Ann. "Resisting Alien Abductions: An Update." *FSR: Flying Saucer Review* 37 (Autumn 1992): pp. 13–14.
3. *The Tujunga Canyon Contacts,* paperback edition, p. 112.
4. Ibid., paperback edition, p. 128.
5. Barron, C. Joseph. MUFON investigative report, interview conducted on January 3, 1990, Pensacola, Florida. Dan Wright. "Current Case Log #900105." *MUFON UFO Journal* no. 264 (April 1990): p. 14.
6. Ibid.
7. For example, veteran researcher John De Herrera (*The Etherean Invasion,* Los Alamitos, Calif: Hwong Publishing, 1978) describes an entity metamorphosed from a ball of light in the presence of abductee Brian Scott. "Balls of light" are also reported in other abduction cases.
8. Druffel, Ann. "Reverend Bailey and the 'Flying Saucer Disease' " in *UFO Abductions,* pt. 2, ed. D. Scott Rogo. New York: Signet/New American Library, 1980, pp. 122–37.
9. Bailey was referred to the UFO medical researcher Richard M. Neal Jr., M.D., for investigation of these claims. Neal's opinion was that Bailey appeared somewhat older than his chronological age. The hospital where Bailey had his surgery in 1963 had slides of tissue taken from his gallbladder. These were examined microscopically by a technical person associated with the Center for UFO Studies (CUFOS), who reported that there was no evident aging apparent in the tissues. The fact that the doctors had made the "aging" statement to Bailey was confirmed by his wife, Anna, but scientific verification is still lacking.
10. Druffel, Ann. "Controversial Entity Photos from California," *MUFON UFO Journal,* nos. 155 and 156 (Jan.–Feb. 1981); "Interpreting the Bailey Case," *MUFON UFO Journal* no. 165, (Nov. 1981); "The Bailey Case Controversy," *MUFON UFO Journal* no. 183. (May 1983); "The Strange Photos of Harrison E. Bailey," *Fate Magazine,* March 1991; London, Michael. "Close Encounters with 'E.T.,' " *Los Angeles Times,*

Calendar Section, June 27, 1982; Druffel and Rogo, *Tujunga Canyon Contacts*, pp. 85–89.

11. Kayton, Myron. "UFO—Fact or Fantasy," *IEEE Aerospace and Electronic Systems*, April 1991, Vol. 6, no. 4.

### Resistance Technique #4: Protective Rage

1. Some UFO colleagues, such as Don Worley and Gordon Creighton in England, researchers I respect highly, might disagree with this statement. They theorize that some UFO abductors are synonymous with demons and devils and are thoroughly evil in nature.

### Resistance Technique #5: Support from Family Members

1. "Joyriding" entities have been described in other well-investigated cases. When the photos of bedroom visitors taken by Rev. Harrison E. Bailey on November 1, 1978, in Pasadena, California, were psychometrized by talented psychic Anita Furdek, she received the strong impression that the two entities Bailey had photographed were young entities, traveling around the universe just for thrills. Tape recordings and transcripts of Furdek's on-site readings are in my files.

2. Jean Moncrief, letter to author, March 1997.

3. Reports of bluish-gray entities, both the "bedroom visitor" type and creatures seen outdoors, are not uncommon, having been reported in the United States and England. For instance, the "Little Blue Men on Studham Common" were described in an early issue (Vol. 13, no. 4, July-August 1967) in *Flying Saucer Review*. An incident involving bluish-gray "bedroom visitors" was also described by an abductee, "Lynn," in *Alien Discussion: Proceedings of Abduction Study Conference at MIT*, edited by Andrea Pritchard et al., Cambridge, Mass.: Cambridge Press, 1994, p. 135.

4. Jean Moncrief, letter to author December 13, 1997.

5. Ibid.

6. Ibid.

7. The Mutual UFO Network (MUFON) is the largest UFO research organization in the world. Inquiries re membership and subscriptions to its monthly research publication, *MUFON UFO Journal*, can be directed to Walter Andrus, International Director, 103 Oldtowne Rd., Seguin, TX 78155.

8. *The Koran*, trans. N. J. Dawood, 4th rev. ed. New York: Viking Penguin, 1974.

## Resistance Technique #6: Intuition

1. Letter to author from "Robert Nolan," January 18, 1992.

2. Copies of most of Nolan's medical records are in both my and Dr. Miller's files and are being treated with the confidentiality they require.

3. During his visits to doctors and hospitalization, physicians confirmed that Nolan's hearing problem problems involved multiple left-sided cranial nerves. The rest of the neurological exam was essentially normal. Nolan had CAT scans and an MRI of his brain and head, which revealed no evidence of strokes, tumor, mass lesion, or foreign body. Two UBOs (Unknown Bright Objects) were in the white matter of the brain on the *right* side, but the radiologist consulted by Dr. Miller explained that such bright spots occur frequently on MRIs and are areas of enhanced magnetic return. "I wish to be very clear about this point," Dr. Miller writes, "They are *not physical objects* but rather some still poorly understood physiologic phenomenon. At least that is how the radiologist explained it to me." (From Dr. John G. Miller's report sent to me December 13, 1997.)

Similar procedures are often performed on experiencers who suspect they have been implanted with "monitoring devices." Sometimes the resultant CAT scans and MRIs reveal the presence of UBOs, leading some abduction researchers and experiencers to accept this as evidence of an actual implant. Since most of these bright spots occur in areas where it would be highly inadvisable to remove them surgically, the suspicion that the UBOs are actual alien implants continues, without any real proof to date. Note that the UBOs in Nolan's MRI were on the *right* side, instead of on the left.

Dr. Miller's interest in this ongoing case continues and he considers Nolan's available medical records to be consistent with the history Nolan has described. He noted how well Nolan's medical records corroborate his verbal account, and feels they establish him as "an accurate historian."

4. Schwarz, Berthold Eric, M.D. *UFO Dynamics: Psychiatric and Psychic Dimensions of the UFO Syndrome.* 2 vols. Moore Haven, Fla.: Rainbow Books, 1983.

## Resistance Technique #7: Metaphysical Methods

1. Most abductees perceive the bedroom visitors and the abduction process as a physical experience that occurs in physical reality. Thus, the frequent comment, "I thought I might be dreaming but was sure it was not a dream," and similar phrases. Much data is being gathered by objective

researchers, however, that strongly indicate that the abduction experience occurs in some kind of as-yet-unidentified state of altered reality.

2. A classic, comprehensive book on this subject is *Altered States of Consciousness,* edited by Charles T. Tart. (New York, London, Sydney, Toronto: John Wiley & Sons, 1969). Since the publication of this seminal work, other scientifically oriented writers have expanded on the concept.

3. Publication by Nevada Aerial Research Group (NARG), July 1990, p. 31. Organization's name has been changed to Leading Edge Research Group, and it is now based in Yelm, Washington.

4. Druffel, Ann and D. Scott Rogo. *The Tujunga Canyon Contacts.* Englewood Cliffs, N.J.: Prentice-Hall, Inc., 1980. Paperback updated edition by Signet Books, 1989.

5. All quotes from Lori Briggs have been taken from audiotapes and transcripts in my files.

6. Dr. Leslie K. Kaeburn, a biophysicist who was noted for his seminal research in implanting monitors in the brains of animals for the first U.S. experiments in space flights was a well-known UFO researcher in the 1960s. He was head of the Los Angeles NICAP Subcommittee. I once asked Dr. Kaeburn what he really thought comprised the UFO phenomenon. After considering the question deeply, he replied, "I don't really know, but I think it must have something to do with light." Although questioned, he did not hypothesize further or give additional details.

7. Bentov, Itzak. *Stalking the Wild Pendulum.* New York: E. P. Dutton Publishers, 1976.

8. OBEs involved with abduction phenomena were also described at the Abduction Study Conference held at MIT, June 13–17, 1992. See *Alien Discussions: Proceedings of the Abduction Study Conference,* eds. Andrea Pritchard, David E. Pritchard, John E. Mack, Pam Kasey, and Claudia Yapp. Cambridge, Mass.: North Cambridge Press, 1994.

9. Ring, Kenneth, Ph.D. *The Omega Project.* New York: William Morrow, 1992.

10. One of the earliest books on the subject is *Out-of-the-Body Experiences* by Robert Crookall, B.Sc., Ph.D. Secaucus, N.J.: The Citadel Press, 1970.

### Resistance Technique #8: Appeal to Spiritual Personages

1. Fox, Rev. Robert J. *The World and Work of the Holy Angels.* Alexandria, S.D.: Fatima Family Apostolate, 1991.

2. A 28-page booklet, *All About Angels*, is available from St. Paul Square, St. Paul, MN 55164.

3. Hufford, David J. *The Terror That Comes in the Night.* Philadelphia: Univ. of Pennsylvania Press, 1982. This excellent book describes "the Old Hag syndrome" as reported by persons in various countries in the Western world. The paranormal experience is very much like that which Timur terms the "Bakhtat" and is also similar to events experienced by abductee Jean Moncrief (see Technique #6).

4. *Alien Discussions,* pp. 235–36. My contributions to this conference can be found on pp. 508–13, in the "Ethics Section," and elsewhere in the *Proceedings.*

5. "Janet," letter to author, n.d., approximately September 1992.

6. Some Catholic theologians advise persons who report seeing "ghosts" or other apparitions to ask them who they are and what they want, in the event they might be souls in trouble.

### Resistance Technique #9: Repellents

1. Ring, Kenneth. *The Omega Project.* New York: William Morrow, 1992.

2. Deborah Goodale Marchand's correspondence with me includes letters dated May 28, 1991; February 3, 1992; February 11, 1992; and March 12, 1998. Quotes from Marchand in the text are derived from these letters.

3. Persse, Isabella Augusta (Lady Gregory). *Visions and Beliefs in the West of Ireland Collected and Arranged by Lady Gregory: With Two Essays and Notes by W. B. Yeats.* New York and London: The Knickerbocker Press, 1920.

4. To me, the idea of carrier craft is very real, having seen this type of UFO as a schoolgirl in 1945 and also in 1962. Accounts of both incidents have been entered into the UFO literature. The term "mother ship" has more or less gone out of fashion among objective researchers, due to the fact that contactees of the 1950s and 1960s used this expression in connection with unsubstantiated stories. "Carrier craft" is a more detached term and is preferred by most scientifically oriented UFO researchers.

5. Jonathan Zuess, *The Natural Prozac Program: How to Use St. John's Wort, the Anti-Depressant Herb.* New York: Harmony Books.

6. See "St. John's Wort," in *Faeries,* described and illustrated by Brian Froud and Alan Lee, edited and designed by David Larkin. New York: Henry N. Abrams/Souvenir Press, 1978.

7. Persse, *Visions and Beliefs in the West of Ireland.* Reference to Rev. Robert Kirk's work in essays by W. B. Yeats included in this book.

8. Reiter, Nicholas A. "The Magnetic Implant Response: A Summary of Experimental Observations." *Bulletin of Anomalous Experience* 2 (June 1991).

9. Persse, *Visions and Beliefs in the West of Ireland,* p. 55.

10. See "Wild Thyme," in Froud, Lee, and Larkin, *Faeries.* As a matter of interest, I have noticed "wild thyme" listed on a few frozen food products. I honestly don't know what advice, if any, to give on this.

**What Abducting Entities in Other Cultures Tell Us About Greys**

1. Dr. Jacques Vallee. *Dimensions: A Casebook of Alien Contact.* New York: Ballantine Books, 1988.

2. From author interviews with Dr. Jacques Vallee.

3. Bullard, Thomas E. "Folkloric Dimensions of the UFO Phenomenon," *Journal of UFO Studies* (1991), pp. 3–40.

4. Creighton, Gordon. "A Brief Account of the True Nature of the 'UFO Entities,' " FSR: *Flying Saucer Review* 29, no. 1 (1983). Reprinted in *FSR* 33 (September 1988).

5. Al-Nahas, Dr. Adil Mosa. Letter to Editor, *FSR* 29, no. 4 (April 1984).

6. Line, Chris. "The Jinn: From A Scientific (?) Viewpoint." *FSR* 34 (December 1989).

7. See FSR: *Flying Saucer Review 1955–1994: An Index,* compiled by Edward G. Stewart, in 1995.

8. Creighton, "Brief Account."

9. Similar sounds and vibrations are described by numerous persons reporting OBEs. All quotes from Timur and text on his experiences are from audiotapes and transcripts in my files.

10. In many abduction scenarios, animals such as owls, large spiders, horses, and other species are sometimes seen at the start of the experience. In the UFO literature, these are often called "screen memories." They apparently divert witnesses' attention until "capture" is accomplished.

11. Gordon Creighton wrote a startling account in *FSR* about a Spanish soldier who was suddenly transported from Manila to Mexico City. See *Flying Saucer Review* 11 (1965). The precise title is not known to me, but that 1965 article and a half-dozen similar, more recent cases in Argentina and Brazil are listed in *FSR Index* (see note 7).

12. Wentz, W. Y. Evans. *The Fairy-Faith in Celtic Countries.* London, New York, Toronto, and Melbourne: Henry Frowde, Oxford University Press, 1911. Wentz studied the faery folklore of Ireland, Scotland, the Isle of Man, Wales, Cornwall, and Brittany. He also found many similarities with beliefs in Native American cultures. In some scholarly books, Evans-Wentz is used as this author's last name, but my library reference search found the book under "w" with no hyphen between "Evans" and "Wentz."

13. Creighton, "Brief Account."

14. Gordon Creighton letter to author, December 2, 1997.

15. The term "interdimensional" as used here describes any state of being that is not normally detectable by the five human senses. Other words synonymous to interdimensional are ultraterrestrial, metaterrestrial, extradimensional, etc. It is also used in the sense that our own vast EM spectrum might possibly contain sources of these "hidden creatures" that are not presently detectable. (See Vallee's clarification earlier in this chapter.) The term implies that creatures from other dimensions interact with humans in an altered state of reality.

16. See "The Killmoulis" in *Faeries*, described and illustrated by Brian Froud and Alan Lee, edited and designed by David Larkin. New York: Harry N. Abrams/Souvenir Press, 1978.

17. Persse, *Visions and Beliefs in the West of Ireland,* Vol. 1, from "Chapter Notes" by Yeats, p. 273.

18. Kirk, Rev. Robert, quoted by W. B. Yeats in *Visions and Beliefs in the West of Ireland,* p. 265.

### The Bitter Controversy

1. Pritchard, Andrea, David E. Pritchard, John E. Mack, Pam Kasey, Claudia Yapp, eds. *Alien Discussions: Proceedings of the Abduction Study Conference Held at MIT.* Cambridge, Mass.: North Cambridge Press, 1994. p. 135. Index references "resistance to aliens" on p. 670.

2. Bryan, C. D. B. *Close Encounters of the Fourth Kind: Alien Abductions, UFOs, and the Conference at MIT.* New York: Alfred A. Knopf, 1995.

3. Pritchard et al., *Alien Discussions,* p. 135.

4. Bullard, Thomas E. "The Sympathetic Ear: Investigators as Variables in UFO Abduction Reports." Mt. Rainier, Md.: Fund for UFO Research, 1995. Pages 54–55 address the resistance issue.

# NOTES

5. Bullard, letter to author, December 28, 1997.

6. Fowler, Raymond. *The Allagash Abductions.* Mill Spring, N.C.: Wildflower Press Bluewater Publishing Co., 1993. This witness's statements about the ineffectiveness of resistance were made to a researcher of my acquaintance at a 1997 private gathering of UFO researchers and abductees.

7. The researcher mentioned in note 6 reports having this conversation with the author of another recent UFO book on abductions, at the same 1997 gathering.

8. Hynek, J. Allen, and Jacques Vallee. *The Edge of Reality.* Chicago: Henry Regnery Company, 1975, pp. 89, 93, 100–8.

9. Fuller, John G. *The Interrupted Journey.* New York: The Dial Press, 1966. Fuller was a well-known journalist who took a scientifically oriented approach toward the UFO subject.

10. Jacobs, David M., Ph.D. *Secret Life.* New York: Simon & Schuster, 1992.

11. White, John. *The Meeting of Science and Spirit.* New York: Paragon Press, 1990. White is the author of many books in the fields of consciousness research and higher human development, including the recently published *What Is Enlightenment?* (New York: Paragon Press, 1995).

12. White, John. Letter to author, November 8, 1997.

13. Ibid.

14. Druffel, Ann. "Can Unwanted UFO Contact Be Resisted?" *BAE* no. 3 (June 1992): pp. 9–11.

15. Boylan, Richard J., Letter to Editor. *BAE* 3 (August 1992).

16. Druffel, Ann. "Resisting Alien Abduction." *MUFON UFO Journal* no. 287 (March 1992): pp. 3–7.

17. Tilly, Virginia M. "Resisting Resisting." *MUFON UFO Journal* no. 292 (August 1992).

18. Ibid.

19. Ibid.

20. Incubi and succubae may be currently interacting with experiencers. Robert Nolan, the abductee who uses Mental and Physical Struggle successfully against greys—but because of his intense curiosity is still troubled by them—recently reported other types of bedroom visitors who fit the description of succubae. The Muslims consider these sex-driven creatures as a type of jinn.

# INDEX

# INDEX

# ABOUT THE AUTHOR

ANN DRUFFEL began investigating UFOs in 1957 with the National Investigations Committee on Aerial Phenomena. She has written for numerous UFO journals, including a bimonthly column for the *Mufon UFO Journal* and significant articles in *International UFO Reporter, UFO Magazine,* and *Flying Saucer Review.* A frequent speaker on the UFO circuit and expert on TV and radio, Druffel is the coauthor of *The Tujunga Canyon Contacts* and a contributor to the *Encyclopedia of UFOs, The Proceedings of the Abduction Study Conference at MIT,* the anthology *UFO Abductions,* and other major works. She is also a veteran psychic researcher, working for ten years for the internationally renowned Mobius Society and pursuing free-lance projects in psychic archeology and other psychic mysteries.